Praise for *Grief and Grit(s)*

"This powerful new memoir is at once a tribute to a beloved mother who died at the height of a global crisis and a clarion call for all of us to look with fresh eyes upon how we take care of one another. Especially our elderly. Surrounded by her devoted family and a barrage of chaotic regulations, Hill dares to take us right into the heart of those terrifying pandemic days as she lays bare the loss and lessons we must all face if we are to do better. Written in vivid prose and with heartbreaking honesty, *Grief and Grit(s)* is a testament to love and healing, a *cri de coeur* for our times."

—Martin Moran, OBIE and LAMBDA Award Winner,
Author of *The Tricky Part* and *All the Rage*

"Grab a cup of coffee, sit in a comfortable chair, and let Marsha Gray Hill tell you her story as if she is seated across from you, talking only to you. You will laugh, you will cry, you will get angry, you will be right there in some of the most intimate moments in the life of the most-godliest person I have ever known. Adaline Gray's legacy will live on through every person her life touched. If you met her, you were never the same. Listen closely as Marsha shares with you the final years, and especially weeks and days, of Adaline's life. I hope it makes you angry, angry enough to do something, even if it's just in your family."

—Jeff Daughtry, Adaline Gray's Pastor, 1992–2000

"*Grief and Grit(s)* is an intimate account of a daughter's journey through love and loss during the COVID-19 pandemic. Marsha Hill's heartfelt memoir explores family, aging, and caregiving, offering essential insights for those facing similar challenges. *Grief and Grit(s)* is a powerful reflection of the power of love, the beauty of life, and a hopeful outlook on the future."

—Tim Richerson, Former President, Rexall Sundown

"*Grief and Grit(s)* offers an intimate portrayal of the journey through Alzheimer's and its profound impact on families. In the challenging context of the COVID pandemic, Marsha Hill's poignant narrative shines a light on the unwavering dedication of caregivers, especially the one who remained steadfast by her loved one's side. A must-read for anyone caring for a family member with Alzheimer's."

—Anna W. Carr, Marketing Consultant,
Long-term Care Southern Assisted Living

"Marsha's heartfelt narrative is a beautiful tribute to her mother and a call to action for society to reevaluate how we care for our aging population. *Grief and Grit(s)* is a moving exploration of love, loss, and the resilience of the human spirit."

—Dr. Gina Loudon, Talk Show Host
and Bestselling Author

"I have known Marsha Hill and her family for over five decades, and it's been a privilege to witness their journey.

Marsha's book, *Grief and Grit(s)*, offers deep insights into the challenges we face as our loved ones age. She courageously confronts the shortcomings in our society's treatment of the elderly, particularly during a pandemic. Marsha's book challenges us all to do better and be better in caring for our elders. It's a profound read that encourages us to reflect on the way we treat the most revered members of our society."

—Rev. Chris Singleton, Free Will Baptist Church

"Truly a heartfelt, loving, and compelling book of a daughter's loss and whose faith helps her find the strength and courage to honor her mother's legacy in the shadow of a global travesty."

—Dr. Linda M Roberts, Owner and Primary Physician
at Synergy Sports Wellness & Performance

"Marsha Hill's *Grief and Grit(s)* is an incredibly moving exploration of love, loss, and resilience in the face of the pandemic's heart-wrenching early days. Her powerful storytelling offers a relatable and compassionate guide to navigating grief, while urging society to better care for one another during times of profound uncertainty and sorrow. A truly exceptional read that will inspire you long after the last page."

— Darci Phillips, M.D., PhD

"I am so proud, and I love Adaline, whom I call 'Great Nine.' This book is so good and so detailed.

—Penn Carter, Marsha Hill's Grandson, Age 8

Grief and Grit(s)

GRIEF and GRIT(S)

A Daughter's Journey of Love and Loss
When the World Was Upside-Down

●●●

MARSHA GRAY HILL

Forefront
BOOKS

Published by Forefront Books.
Distributed by Simon & Schuster.

Library of Congress Control Number: 2023917768

Print ISBN: 978-1-63763-232-1
E-book ISBN: 978-1-63763-233-8

Cover Design by George Stevens, G Sharp Design LLC
Interior Design by PerfecType, Nashville, TN

To Mama,
Who inspired me to write this story,
Who lived this story,
Who is this story.

Contents

Foreword
by Brittany Hill Carter

Taking care of my grandma in her final days was one of the greatest privileges of my life. To be a part of a loved one's journey into stillness and death is a strange but also beautiful thing. In my job as a physician assistant (PA) who takes care of patients with malignant blood disorders, I am often around people who are in the process of actively dying. I have been a part of many devastating patient encounters when bad news is delivered and hospice decisions are made. I have been brought to tears when a young mom whom I have only known for a few days hears there is nothing more that can be done for her.

Although patients have sometimes felt like family and I try to treat them like family, there is nothing that compares to losing a family member of your own. The emotions run so much deeper. Somehow amidst the chaos and complexity of my grandma actively dying from COVID-19, I was at peace. I have been trying to figure out why, and I think it is mostly that I knew my grandma was at peace. She never feared death because of her deep faith in God. This is not something that I assume. This is something I know for sure because she said this with some regularity. She lived a long, beautiful life. I still feel a hint of guilt wishing I could have helped more or done more, but then I realize that by thinking that way, I am acting as if I am in control of these things. The reality is that for people of faith or who have a deep sense of spiritualty, God is in control.

I wasn't at my grandma's side the moment she passed, which still bothers me a bit. I left her apartment to go pump breast milk to store in the refrigerator for my infant son, but also to get a little sleep and get a break from the N95 mask that was cutting into my face. I wish I had been there, but I know my grandma didn't mind. I can just hear her sweet voice saying to me, "Honey, you just go ahead and get milk for that baby and rest and leave me to get on to Jesus."

My grandma taught me and showed me what it meant to be a healer and a caregiver. My grandfather had type 1 diabetes and needed insulin injections multiple times per day. I would watch her gently give these to him, and one day I asked her if I could try. She let me practice on an orange for a while before I was allowed to do the real thing. My poor grandfather let a ten-year-old give him his insulin injections! This became a regular thing when I would arrive at their house.

My grandma took care of my grandfather with such grace and kindness. It was never a chore for her because it came from such a loving place. We called her an honorary nurse because she took care of everyone it seemed—the

neighbors, church members, friends, relatives, coworkers—
and probably even a few strangers here and there.

Some of my grandma's DNA must have skipped my
mom and come straight to me. My grandma would always
say that she "was born tired and had a relapse." This pretty
much sums me up! Bless her heart, she lacked organization and any Type A personality traits. If you opened up
any given drawer in her house, you might find a random
assortment of things: an empty plastic bag, a lone clothes-
pin, a lollipop, a dollar bill, a receipt from five years ago,
a spoon, and a real ponytail she had saved from when my
mom had a dramatic hair cut back in high school. Open up
any drawer in my own house, and you will find a similar
situation. Despite my best efforts to stay organized with my
busy life with three children, I can't quite pull it together.

Now this brings me to my mom, who is the author
of this phenomenal book. My mom is a force! While my
grandma and I would be late to any gathering and miss
deadlines, my mom is the epitome of "on top of it." I know
many of you reading this book are quite likely Type A
and organized, but my mom takes it to another level. She
thinks about every single tiny detail and is an event planner
extraordinaire. Each regular family holiday turns into an
epic event. Fourth of July, for example, is not just a weekend with family, some burgers, and pool time. My mom
plans and executes treasure hunts for the kids where the
kids dress as pirates and parade down to the beach where
they hunt for treasure (that she has secretly hidden under
the sand). There are pie eating contests, decorations galore,

multiple cakes, video slide shows, fireworks displays (run by my dad but orchestrated by her), matching T-shirts for everyone to wear, family photo sessions with coordinated outfits, Fourth of July themed floats in the pool, and red white and blue everything! To top it all off is the food situation. I call it a "situation" because it is something to be reckoned with.

My mom loves her family more than anything in the world. You will never meet anyone else who puts her family first the way that she does. She does so much for all of us, and it is out of love rather than obligation. To know my mom is to love her. People gravitate towards her. If I had a quarter for every time a friend of mine has said, "Can your mom adopt me?" I would have a room full of quarters (as I am writing this, I realize that the "if I had a quarter" expression is one I stole from my grandma).

The funny thing is, while my mom wishes she was more like her mom, I wish I was more like my mom. We all desire to have qualities that we don't have, but what I think we don't realize is how similar we are to one another than we are different. In this book, my mom makes the point that she is very different from her mom. Yes, in many ways this is true. But what my mom doesn't point out (and maybe doesn't quite realize), is that she is like my grandma in so many ways. My mom has a heart for giving and loving. Yes, she loves her family, but she also loves others. She still sends regular meals to the parents of her favorite massage therapist who tragically died two years ago. She recently sent money to a chef she met thirty years ago in a Japanese restaurant (and hasn't seen since) because she saw his social media post that he was having difficulty getting good in-home care for his invalid daughter. My mom didn't tell you these things in her book because that is not who she is, but she, too, has a servant's heart. She, too, raised us in a gentle manner with few rules and lots of love. She loves and loves, and when it seems like there is no more love to give, she loves some more. She is far more like Adaline Gray than she knows.

When I was fresh out of PA school, I was so eager to help and work. My first years working extremely long hours in the hospital taught me so many things. I learned that I truly loved taking care of patients and loved getting to know them on a personal level. I loved getting to know their family and friends and their hopes and fears. I also learned that I wouldn't and couldn't sleep until the work was done. I learned that I am a perfectionist when it comes to taking care of patients. I learned that the more time I gave my patients, the later I stayed at work and the less time I had for myself. I learned that I had to work a lot faster than was naturally comfortable for me. I learned that chatting with a lonely patient for twenty minutes about her grandkids made me late for rounds with the physician. I learned that long hours, perfectionism, and a chronically understaffed working environment were a recipe for burnout. I burned out quickly. Our medical system is flawed in that it often doesn't (or can't) take good enough care of medical providers, who in turn then can't give enough time and energy to their patients or to their families at home. This book highlights some of our medical system's shortcomings.

Although I didn't work much in the early days of the COVID-19 pandemic, I worked enough to get a sense of what providing care during that time felt like in our department. I felt so sad seeing patients alone in their hospital rooms. Many of our patients spend over a month in the hospital at a time getting chemotherapy treatments. This is no easy task with an army of friends and family visiting, but with not even one visitor, it seems practically impossible. Patients did it because at the end of the day, what choice did they have? I worried about their mental states. I worried about the mental states of all of us. I know that countless numbers of people worldwide died in ways and in situations that were far from ideal. My grandma was one of those people, and it ripped all of our hearts right open. Her story needs to be told. Your stories need to be told too.

Introduction

Of all the ways my mother could have died, it shouldn't have been like that.

I still have nightmares about seeing her in that little room, watching her struggle for every breath. Of course, there's the whole medical side of things—the panic, the confusion, the desperation, and the struggle to get any sort of help or support in May of 2020. But as frustrating as it is to think about the things I couldn't have planned for, things completely beyond my control, I can't help but reflect on the choices I did make. Did I do the right thing? Did I fight hard enough? Was I too scared, too timid, too weak? At the end of it all, should I have been there holding her hand?

If anyone ever deserved anything, my mother deserved to pass from this life in peace, surrounded by the countless folks who loved and adored her. But the cold, hard fact is that Lanie Adaline Gray died in the company of the one brave caretaker who refused to leave her side. No children, grandchildren, or even great-grandchildren were there.

None of the hundreds of individuals she'd impacted as a teacher, a mentor, a mother, and a friend.

That image stings. I guess when I envisioned the end of her life, I always thought someone like her would go surrounded by all the people who loved and adored her.

Not a lot of people think about how they're going to die. It's not a comfortable subject or something you casually bring up at a dinner party. We don't really like to think about our loved ones dying either, which is pretty strange if you take a moment to stop and think about it. All of us are born to parents. And eventually, those parents are going to die—more often than not before their children. This is just how life goes. Sure, we watch our parents age, begin to slow down, forget things . . . But we don't ever want to think about the end or what that may mean for our busy lives.

My mother has always been "Mama," and she spent her whole life teaching, whether that was at the pulpit, in a Sunday school program, or even recreating *The Sound of Music* with my children on the stairs. I don't know why I thought those lessons would stop when she died. I learned more about her life, myself, and the nature of humanity losing her to COVID-19 on that sweltering May morning than I ever have anywhere else.

But the loss didn't start or end there. I'd been losing Mama long before that, back when she started wandering, misplacing her car keys, and blaming the "gremlins" every time her mind slipped. As traumatic as it was to watch an elderly parent die during a global pandemic, the smaller, more subtle losses over years of dementia and Alzheimer's are a slower, agonizing grief.

COVID was uncontrollable and unpredictable. There was nothing any of us could have done to prepare for it. There's nothing that prepares you for taking care of an elderly parent, either. No one talks about what it's like to become the caretaker for someone who once took care of you. We all know that old age is waiting for everyone, but even though death is something *all of humanity* has in common, you can't prepare for or control it, either.

I'm a planner by nature. I always have been, and I imagine I always will be. I'm the kind of woman who has all the grandkids' Christmas stockings stuffed in July, that crazy lady who sorts everything by color, theme, and adorable matching outfits. As a mother of five kids, I've always had to be three steps ahead, and when Mama started deteriorating, my mind went into emergency overdrive. Maybe it was just habit. Or maybe I was trying to protect myself from the pain waiting ahead.

Before Mama died, I'd been planning her funeral for years, listening to her wishes for what she would wear, which songs would be played, who would speak, and even what sorts of decorations would best represent the amazing life she lived. But there's only one thing I can plan on for my own sendoff, and that's the inscription on my tombstone: "*That's what Marsha Hill got for planning.*"

Nothing about Mama's funeral went the way I'd so painstakingly prepared it to go. All the organization, prep work, preordering, and boxes of carefully customized decorations did nothing to ease the pain of losing her the way we did. It didn't do anything for the guilt and second-guessing either. As much as I tried to control every detail of the process, I was left stunned. Lonely. Adrift in a sea of pain and confusion. Looking back, I don't think any amount of preparation would have changed that.

In the end, Mama didn't get the send-off she deserved. That's part of the reason I wanted to write this book—to honor her, her selflessness, and the incredible woman she was. There are a lot of people who think the world of their mothers—that their mom is the "best mom"—but when I say my mom was perfect, I truly mean it. And if you want to disagree or argue with me, well, I guess you're going to have to keep reading.

Maybe "perfect" isn't a metric we can use to judge anyone's character (I've always been one to embellish a good story), and it's near impossible to measure the raw human impact that anyone makes on the world. However, if the inpouring of *hundreds* of letters, cards, stories, and messages from the folks Mama touched mean anything, I would say they're a pretty good indicator of the life she lived. Everything my mother did was for other people in a spirit of true love, trust, and humanity, and that might have been a part of why she died the way she did.

But before we get into the full story, I want to be very clear about what this book is and what it isn't. First and foremost, this book is *not* a political statement. This isn't a book about shame, blame, or pointing fingers. None of this is about "us versus them" or calling out specific individuals.

A few names have been redacted and changed, and that's very intentional too. There's enough hatred and pain surrounding the thousands of COVID and COVID-related deaths. There's no need to rip open those wounds.

This book *is* a record of the facts surrounding my mother's life and her death. My Granddaddy Gray was always an avid recordkeeper. Every day, he would jot something down—even if it was only a few lines—and he was the one who inspired me to pick up that habit. I couldn't be more grateful to him because of it. In the chaos of so much pain, fear, and loss, it's important that we have eyewitness accounts of what actually happened, especially when it relates to those whose voices are so often cast aside or overlooked.

One of the craziest things about this time was seeing the best and the worst of humanity. There were heroes everywhere, ordinary people who chose to show up in extraordinary ways. There were also those who chose differently, posts that were abandoned, oaths of care and courage that weren't honored. Having all experienced this, we know what a time of fear and confusion 2020 was, and that's why I don't believe any part of this story should be about judgment. What happened, happened, and I hope that, as we take the time to share these stories and unravel the truth, our judgment can mature into understanding and gratitude.

What's lost is lost, and there's no going back. There was bravery, there was cowardice, and as I mentioned, I'm still haunted by my own decisions years later. The greatest tragedy, however, would be to have lived through the age of COVID and learned nothing as a community.

This is a book to honor Lanie Adaline Gray, her life, her love, and the lessons she continues to impart to us every day. I hope this project affords her even the smallest bit of honor and the respect she deserves—the honor and respect she wasn't afforded when she died.

This is also a book about the COVID pandemic, what we saw, experienced, and lived through as individuals, families, and communities. This generation has never seen this kind of collective trauma on such a massive scale. We need to be talking about it. We have whole generations of missing people, children who spent foundational years learning from a distance, parents who had to scramble to learn how to homeschool their kids while struggling to manage their own full-time jobs . . . Everyone has a story to tell, and by sharing our stories, we connect with one another on a deeper, human level. We can laugh together. We can cry together. We can be grateful, celebratory, angry—and just maybe, we can start to help one another heal.

But most importantly, this is a book about advocating for the elderly, our culture surrounding senior citizens, and what we need to do better. More than anything else, COVID has shown me that our generational gap has become a chasm of empathy, care, and understanding. I wish I could tell you I have solutions. I wish I could tell you I have all the answers. But just because we don't have everything figured out doesn't mean we can ignore this problem. Our elderly are some of the most neglected and vulnerable people in our community, and this is why respect, care, and dignity need to stay a topic of conversation.

Caring for an elderly parent is a specific stage of life that most people would rather not talk about. Everyone loves baby books such as, *What to Expect When You're Expecting*, *What to Expect the First Year*, *Guide to a Healthy Pregnancy* . . . But no one's giddily gifting any guides about taking responsibility for an aging family member—maybe even a dying family member. Sure, we swap tips about diapering babies, but the conversation takes a drastic turn when it comes to your own parents' losing control of their bowels.

Unlike the joys and trials of watching a baby grow, with an aging family member, the complications only get worse, and it can be a steep, downhill plunge. You sit there and watch in real time as a grown, fully functioning member of society regresses to the helplessness of a child. No one warned me about the financial, physical, and psychological demands of this duty that many people get, but no one asks for. No one sat me down and had "the talk" about what to do when my mother's mind was so far gone, she started weeping for her long-dead parents.

Believe me when I say that nothing in the world can prepare you for that.

The conversation isn't comfortable. And it shouldn't be. When we think about the fact that the ones we love get old and die, we also have to face the reality that we ourselves are, one day, going to get old and die. That's a hard enough pill to swallow when things are normal, never mind having to deal with it throughout the looming pandemonium of a worldwide pandemic.

But this is why we need to be opening ourselves up to these hard conversations. As loved ones grow and age, how can we help them through these transitions? How will we care for them with the immediate and demanding responsibilities of our own busy lives? And how can we navigate the treacherous waters of aging, sickness, and dying with grace and dignity?

Like I said, I don't have any answers. Truly, I wish I knew a cure-all solution—some sort of magic wand I could wave to make this a simple, easy process. But just like every birth is different, every death is different as well. Maybe by making these conversations less taboo, being honest about this difficult reality, and sharing the ups and downs of our own stories, we can be a little bit more empathetic, better equipped for the dark parts of life we can't control.

Yes, this is a book about Mama. But this is also a book about me, what I've learned, how I've grown, and the beautiful (sometimes painful) lessons my mother has taught me at every stage of her life. But these aren't just my stories. They're *her* stories—the stories I share with my family, my friends, and the world. Stories are how we connect with one another, grow together, and learn to love deeper. Stories are a part of what makes us human.

My hope in sharing this story is that it touches you in some way. While every one of us has been affected differently by the COVID pandemic, we all lived through it. We all have parents, too, and eventually, we're all going to lose them in some way or another. We all know what it's like to fear, and we all know the feeling of taking on responsibility we never asked for.

No matter where you've been, where you are now, or how this book touches you, I hope it starts a discussion, a conversation about how we can take these collective experiences and use them to build a better, brighter future for all generations.

The fact is, life goes on. Over the months I pored over this prologue, I watched the attitude of the pandemic begin to shift. Depending on where you are, you could say that things "lightened up." Restrictions were lifted, masks came off, and lives quickly started to settle into a "new normal"— whatever that's supposed to mean.

I'm sure things will continue to settle, but at this point in time, the transformation feels strange. Eerie, almost. While settling back into what we remember of our pre-pandemic lives feels like a breath of fresh air, it's bizarre to remember the fear and the panic, the lockdowns, constant news streams, and apocalyptic scrambles for single rolls of toilet paper. Seeing people unmasked, walking the streets, part of me wonders, *Did this really happen? Was it all some mass, fevered dream? Are we all going to sit here and pretend that* none of this *was real?*

Of course, I'm not blaming anyone for not *wanting* to dwell on collective trauma. When someone asks you to go back into a warm, fuzzy memory, I doubt many people are thinking about months upon months locked up in tiny apartments. However, if we don't talk about what happened—the cowards, the heroes, the mistakes, the triumphs, the losses, and the victories—we're going to miss out on everything we can learn from it. And that, in my opinion, would be adding insult to injury.

That's why these stories have to come to life. That's why *Mama's* story has to come to life. She wasn't just a number or one of the thousands upon thousands of elderly lives the virus claimed. Adaline Gray was an extraordinary woman who lived an extraordinary life. She saw a national economic depression as well as a world war, witnessed the first man landing on the moon, and stuck around long enough to use a smartphone. Through her ministry, she shaped the futures of countless children around the world, along with living to see fifteen of her great-grandchildren join our family and continue her legacy. There are few lives on this earth as rich and full as Mama's. In sickness and in health, in poverty and riches, she exemplified the kind of woman I strive to be every day. There is so much to mourn—so many things I wish could have gone differently—but also so much to celebrate and learn from her memory. In every season, Mama lived bravely, loved fiercely, and chose to see the best in people, even when they failed to show the same courtesy to her. Until her dying breath, she was caring for others.

I'd always imagined Mama passing on to heaven peacefully and comfortably in her bed, surrounded by family and adoring loved ones. In the end, though, she was gasping for air, too weak to eat, drink, or even hold up her head. I thank God every day that her one stalwart caretaker stayed by her side, and her own granddaughter had to be the one to pronounce her dead. A group of strangers brought her out of her tiny apartment. She'd preached countless sermons over the course of her life, but a pastor she didn't even know muttered her last rites in a parking lot.

It was a strange time. A time of fear, confusion, and collective anguish that this generation had never seen. Rich and poor, old and young, COVID touched all of us, and like death, it's now an experience we all have in common.

But as horrible as Mama's death was, there is so much more to her life. This isn't just a story about the pandemic. It's also a story of joy, peace, and love—of a "perfect" woman who left behind a legacy far greater than any of us can understand. This book, these lessons, and this discussion are part of that legacy. Wherever, whenever, and however you may be reading these stories, it's my sincere prayer that something in these pages touches you, if not through a personal connection to Mama, then a resolve to do better to take care of the ones who once cared for us.

My mother's life and death are reflections of who we are, who we continue to be not only as individuals, but as a greater society. And in her story, I hope we can find the forgiveness, absolution, and love she modeled while she was here on earth.

If you're like me, sitting here in the wake of the destruction and loss, wondering what in the heck you're supposed to do with all this, know you're not alone. I might not have answers, but together, we can find a way to move forward. Let's tell our stories. Let's share our losses. And as we grow and learn from the triumphs and the tragedies, maybe—just maybe—we can begin to heal.

The End

I never thought I'd go out like this. For all we'd seen and survived, I'd never envisioned my husband, Gregg, and me spending these critical days—maybe the scariest, most uncertain days of our lives—huddled together in a tiny twin bed.

For the sake of context, it's important to know that Gregg is six-foot-six. The air conditioning was out in our bedroom, and even in the early days of May 2020, the Florida heat was far from pleasant, which drove us to take refuge in our boys' tiny bunkroom. Still, my husband and I held each other. We didn't know what to think. We didn't know what to say. After all my efforts, planning, and scrambling, there was nothing I could do to fix things.

My COVID test was the first to come through, and it was positive. I didn't know what that meant for me. I didn't know what that meant for my husband. I didn't know what that meant for my elderly mother, two minutes down the street, fighting for her life.

Gregg and I nestled close that night, despite the muggy heat. "If we go down," he said, "we go down together."

I didn't have much to say to that. My head was a whirlwind, my thoughts tangled and crazy. The *world* was tangled and crazy, so much so that people were pushing and shoving their way through grocery stores to buy up the last scraps of toilet paper. Nobody could have imagined what a global pandemic would do to our communities and the wide world around us. None of us could have predicted the raw level of fear.

Simply knowing I had the virus was horrible in its own right. I was utterly exhausted though it's hard to tell if it was COVID-related or brought on by the sheer, grueling stress of trying to keep my mother alive the last few weeks. As I lay there in that tiny twin bed, breathing heavily, wondering what the positive test meant for me and the love of my life sleeping beside me, I almost had to laugh because I had no energy to cry anymore.

After everything we'd been through, I couldn't believe this would be how it ended.

I was terrified to get the results of my COVID test. I hadn't had any symptoms, but my mother was terribly ill, and we needed to know for sure if she or anyone in contact with her was positive for the virus. The moment I opened that email and saw the letter P in positive, I knew where I'd been infected—and I knew what my condition meant for my mother. We'd taken all the precautions we could, wearing masks, airing out her tiny rooms, and keeping everything clean. But after the lockdown began, there was only one place in the world where I could have picked up the virus, only one place where anyone outside our household went in and out.

Mama's apartment.

It's one thing to fret about your own mortality. This was months after the initial COVID outbreak in the US, the time when we didn't know exactly what the sickness was, how it spread, or how to stop it. These were the days where you couldn't flip to a single channel without some footage or banner about new precautions or the running death toll and talking heads blabbering on about failures and conspiracies as if this state of fear and chaos could be distilled down into something as simple as a political rivalry.

Sitting there, sweating in that tiny bed, I was terrified, not just for myself, but for my mama. If I'd tested positive, there was no doubt she was positive too. And at ninety-one years of age, I knew in my heart that the results beneath her name would be her death sentence.

As I mentioned, I'm a meticulous journal keeper. I still have my notes from that final week. There's one line in particular that stands out to me: *"The images of her breathing will never leave me."*

The rasping. The rattling. The look in her eyes when she was too weak to lift her head off her pillow or even swallow any of her food.

"I've put Mama through so much," I wrote. *"I'm just trying to get her better."*

Most of what I remember about those blurry days is being so, *so* tired.

I was exhausted. I'd been fighting for so long. Not just fighting back the inevitable, trying to care for my mother with the love, respect, and dignity she deserved, but trying to fight a disease no one knew how to fight—trying to fight an entire medical system that would sooner throw her away and dismiss her as another number than make any effort to save her life. And, yes, my mother was elderly. She was frail and had struggled with dementia for the last twelve years. But she was also *my* mother—my "baby" and my charge. The doctors may have given up on her, citing the inevitability or their need to triage their patients. But I wasn't ready to give up on my mama. The fire in my belly wouldn't let me.

My mother had faithfully served others her whole life, tending to the sick and even styling hair for the deceased so they looked peaceful for their loved ones, lying in their coffins. She was kind, considerate, and agreeable to a fault, the kind of woman who spent her free time shuttling the poor and disabled back and forth from church events. I knew perfectly well that my mother was elderly and had no hope of being any doctor's top priority, but I wouldn't let her be discarded as a number. She was a beautiful soul. She deserved better than that.

There's a strange thing that happens when your parent becomes your child. And I don't mean that ironically or tongue in cheek. My father had died years before, and when Mama's mind and body began to fail, I was the one who cared for her as her health deteriorated. I was the one who stood and watched as she went from the strong, capable woman who'd raised me to a child I'd never known—someone confused, vulnerable, frightened, and at times, paper-thin. This was the time, I think, I loved my mother more fiercely and truly than I'd ever loved her before. She was more than my mama. She was my baby. And if you've ever known the love of a mother or felt that love yourself, you know how powerful it can be.

Mama and I had a strange connection those last few years, the kind of connection that makes mothers flinch when they feel their child has skinned a knee or wake up in the cold sweat of nightmares with a "hunch" that something's wrong. Before Mama passed, I knew it was coming.

Somehow, crammed in that tiny bed, I fell into a fitful sleep, only to be jerked awake at 3 a.m. I couldn't breathe. It was like something was sitting on my chest. I tried the breathing and relaxation techniques my doctor had taught me, but even those didn't help. Whether it was the anxiety, the COVID symptoms, or my connection to Mama, I'll never know.

Either this is the virus, I thought, *or Mama is dying.*

Does she know? I wondered. Even in the throes of her own struggle, I could feel her thinking about me. *As a mother, is she worried sick?*

That night, sitting in the darkness, I began to talk to her. I assured her that Gregg would take care of me, that my brother Eddie and I would take care of each other, and that everything would be fine.

"There's no reason to worry," I told her. "We're OK. You can let go."

Even before I made the call, I knew she was gone. Sometime around 7 a.m. that morning, I rang up Mama's caretaker, Regina, to confirm what had happened. Mama had passed sometime between 3 a.m. and 6 a.m. that morning, during the time I was talking to her. She'd gone without a sound. Regina, who'd been lying in the bed beside her, had gotten up to use the bathroom, only to return and find Mama had passed. All things considered, that didn't surprise me one bit. If there was one thing she hated, it was being a bother or inconveniencing anyone. She had been gravely ill for two weeks, but it had only been one day since we received her COVID diagnosis.

At first, I was overwhelmed with frustration. I'm a mother of five, and mothers are supposed to fix things. When my mama became unable to take care of herself, she became *my* baby. Isn't it every mother's nightmare to be unable to care for, protect, and provide for their child?

By nature, I'm a fixer. I'm a planner, a provider—dare I say the "matriarchal type." But no matter how hard I tried, this was something I just couldn't fix. It was completely out of my control, and Lord knows I *love* to be in control.

I have recurring nightmares about being unable to get milk for my children. In these dreams, my babies are mewling and squalling. They're so hungry, they're in pain. And I run around, frantically, trying to do something—anything—to get them something to eat.

It was that same feeling of helplessness that had been creeping over me like a dark shadow the weeks prior to

Mama's death. As her condition steadily worsened, and it became apparent that there was nothing we could do to help her, that horrible, sickening feeling got worse. I'd come to terms with the fact that someone I loved so dearly and desperately was aging and would eventually pass on. It was the fact that there was nothing I could do to help her. I had no way to process the fear, confusion, and pain that ate me up from the inside out.

But after the wave of powerlessness, the anger, frustration, and grief, there came a strange peace.

"She's no longer suffering," I wrote in my journal. *"I'll miss her forever."*

It's hard to grasp how two things can be true at once. The day she died, I was overwhelmed with sadness, but there was also a strange sense of release, like finally reaching the top of a mountain after a grueling, uphill climb. For the first time in weeks, I could catch my breath. Mama was gone, and there was absolutely nothing I could do about it, nothing *left* for me to do about it. I'd been operating frantically in fight-or-flight mode for so long. And now, there was nothing left to fight for.

But of course, that's when the guilt of the aftermath settled in. When it came to caring for Mama and making decisions on her behalf, I couldn't help but feel like everything I did was wrong. Like, somehow, I'd failed her.

In situations like these, there's no way to win, no way to climb in bed the next night with the peace of knowing you made the right decision, no one to affirm or comfort you for doing absolutely everything you could. You'll always live with the guilt of the *what-ifs*—what if you'd done something better, faster, or even sooner? You'll play out those scenarios for endless nights as you stare up at your darkened ceiling, and no matter how hard you try, you'll never get the answers you're looking for.

For me, this has been a necessary part of the grieving process. Things happened so quickly, too fast for me even to be present in Mama's last moments. Reliving these blurry days, hyperfixating on every junction and decision, has helped me put those scattered pieces back together in a way that, eventually, just might make sense.

I know this guilt isn't healthy, and it certainly isn't anything I would ever wish on anyone. But I also hope that someday these emotions will become a little less painful, a little less hot to the touch. It's taking me a long time to make sense of things and find forgiveness, but I want to give myself that time with the same patient kindness that Mama always showed me. There's pain in perspective. But there's also wisdom and progress—the chance of doing things a little better than we did last time.

When Mama finally departed, the peace I felt from her was just as real as the body she'd left behind. She'd released her earthly burdens, and in her own gentle way, she'd given me permission to release mine. I had to let her go, to assure her that she didn't have to stay with us any longer. The freedom of her spirit was also the freedom of my soul. I, too, had to move on, even though I had no idea what that would look like or where to even begin.

I'd fought for my mother so hard and so long for so many years. Sitting there in the dark, crying my eyes out as I struggled to breathe, I couldn't help but wonder . . .

What now?

What could any of this possibly mean?

2

My Girl

'll bet you've heard someone in your life say they wish they could build a time machine and "go back to the way things were." Maybe they think a different time was a simpler one or that by returning to some part of their life they've mostly forgotten then all their problems would magically resolve.

I think I've lived long enough to know better. When I think about my past, my childhood, and "the way things were," of course, the rosy memories come up first. I was a child. Things *were* simpler—they always are when you're not paying taxes or worried about gas prices—but that's not to say anything was better or worse.

It's pretty narrow-minded to think that any particular place in history was without its own troubles. Of course, they probably weren't the same troubles you and I face today, but you have to consider that all experiences are relative to the person experiencing them. A medieval peasant farmer probably wasn't stressing out about filing their taxes every April, but they sure were worried about the bubonic plague. It may seem like an ancestor in the roaring twenties lived a fabulous, glamorous life, but you also have to consider their access to things we take for granted every day—things such as toilet paper, pain relievers, and tampons.

If you plan on using a time machine to find a place where people were happier, life was simpler, or things made more sense, I'm sorry to say you're not going to get what you're looking for. Every generation has its own challenges. Every life has its ups and its downs.

Now, don't get me wrong. If there were a time machine available, I would absolutely use it. (Honestly, who wouldn't?) But if I had access to that kind of technology, I wouldn't go back to relive experiences or search for greener pastures. I would go back to get Mama's stories from her own eyes.

Children have a hard time understanding that their parents have their own histories, lives, and experiences that existed before they were born. Growing up, it's something you never really think about. You're so busy living your own story, you don't pay a lot of attention to your parents' stories. Even as an adult with my own family, I didn't give much thought to my parents' histories until it was too late.

What I know of my mama's early life is random and scattered. It's like trying to put together an old jigsaw puzzle when you know you don't have all the pieces. When I was a girl, my parents were busy working. My brother and I would ask them about stories from their past, but they were busting their hides day after day to create a new story for us. They were young, poor, and hardworking. They hadn't taken the time to reflect on the span of their lives and what their memories meant. That came as they got older and slowed down, and by the time that happened, I was busy juggling five kids of my own.

One of the greatest things my kids have done for my husband, Gregg, and me was to purchase a service that periodically sends us a list of questions about our past, both as a couple and before we were married. We answer the prompts via email, and at the end of the year, the company gathers our responses into a book for our children and grandchildren.

Now that we're a bit older (I'm not going to lie and say we're less busy), the things that have happened in our lives— the events that challenged us, shaped us, and brought us to where we are now—make a little more sense than they did in the moment. Maybe that's wisdom, or maybe wisdom is just perspective. Whatever the case, it's been nice to have an intentional, diligent place where my husband and I can reflect on and record specific instances from our childhood. The world was very different back then, but it wasn't just time that made a difference. Making money, having children, sickness, death, success, failure, moving out of your hometown—all of it changes you and becomes a part of your story. And as you get older, you start to see the value in those little "random" events that stick out in your mind.

I wish I had done a better job recording Mama and Daddy's stories. I wish I had sat down and taken intentional time to hear them directly from her. But, like most things, you only miss what you don't have the moment you need it. Now that Mama is gone, I'm scrambling to put together the pieces she left behind.

And by most standards, I'm pretty lucky. I have photographs, notes, and letters from her childhood, which is more than most can say. But no matter how much I discover or piece together, there's always something missing. The more I uncover, the more frustrating the gaps in the narrative get. In the process of writing this book, I've dragged countless relics out of the dusty darkness into the light of day.

It *is* like trying to put together a jigsaw puzzle, one of the old, yellowing ones that lives in a plastic bag because the box was long-lost at a bygone Christmas party. You dig it out, start working the outline, and when it finally seems like you're starting to make sense of the picture, you realize there are gaps in the story that will never be filled, bits and pieces of her life that are lost forever. For all your effort, that puzzle is never going to be finished. For a perfectionist, that grates on me like no one's business. As a grieving daughter, it leaves me with an aching sadness that words can't describe.

If I had a time machine, I wouldn't go back to Mama's childhood. I would go back to a time where I could sit down with her, just she and I, sipping Pepsi-Cola (her all-time favorite) through straws on a beautiful Carolina day. I would ask her about the gaps in the story. I would laugh and cry with her as she dug deep in her memory for all that she'd lived, loved, and lost. But most of all, I would take the time to just sit there and listen. In silence, I would honor every anecdote, no matter how funny, tragic, or seemingly insignificant, with my time and attention. I would take notes, and I would weave those notes into stories. And then I would share those stories with the people who love her so they, too, could have even the smallest glimpse of the beautiful picture that was my mother's life.

Yes, the beginning of Mama's story is a little scattered from my perspective. But as much as I wish I had more, I'm extremely grateful for the pieces I do have. And like just about everything in my life, I feel called to do the best with what I've got.

In the end, it's not just *the* story that matters. It's *her* story.

Lanie Adaline Hall was born in Sandy Bottom, North Carolina, on September 7, 1928, to Frank and Lanie Hall. Back then, living on the cutting edge of a new century had a completely different meaning. Mama's father was a sharecropper, and with four sisters and one brother in the family, they grew up dirt poor.

That's not just an expression. Mama spoke about literally being able to see the dirt through the planks in the floor of the rinky-dink house they grew up in. One thing she emphasized was always being cold. She and her sisters would bunch together at night, huddling against one another to stay warm. They grew their own food, and her grandmother would sew all of the children's clothes. This was the time families lived closer together for obvious reasons. No one had money for babysitters or hired help. You had your family, and your family was all you had. From a young age, Mama was expected to help with everything, working in the gardens, picking cotton in the fields, watching her younger siblings, and taking care of chores such as sewing and cooking.

The sisters of the family were closer than any sisters I've ever seen. Mama had distinct memories of the girls going to the bathroom together, holding hands and singing to one another while they sat on the toilet. And without iPhones or *Reader's Digest*, it makes perfect sense. She and her older sister, Helen, were two years apart. The two shared a bed and were practically inseparable. "If I could just reach Helen's feet at night," Mama would say, "I knew my feet would be warm."

One day, the girls heard a commercial about "contented cows giving better milk." This was probably some advertisement for some sort of feed or farm product (we're talking about rural eastern North Carolina, after all), but the sisters took this to mean that the cow could be contented any which way. So naturally, they decided that whatever made them happy was bound to make the cow happy. They went out to the barn and started singing to it, all together, hoping to get the finest milk in Craven County. I guess we'll never know whether or not the singing worked, but it is a nice visual. If I were that cow, I think I would have appreciated it.

The highlight of the year was when her father would trek the long miles to the nearest store and bring back supplies. On his trip, he would buy a Coca-Cola for each child; that was their yearly treat. Until her dying day, Mama loved soda (she later became a Pepsi-Cola girl, but that's beside the point). To her, it meant something different. I think there are very few people who enjoy a simple can of soft drink the way she did. Between their yearly Coca-Cola treat, she talked about gnawing on raw sweet potatoes as a snack.

You could say Mama's childhood was backward or Podunk, just a part of being raised in the country, but that's never been the whole story. Even I have to remind myself that Mama grew up during the Great Depression. Poverty wasn't just a North Carolina thing; it was an *everywhere* thing.

Another memorable fact about my mother was that she never liked onions. She couldn't stand the taste or even the smell of them. When she was young, her Aunt Hazel, a city girl, had come to visit, bearing gifts—Coca-Cola and one of the newest fad trinkets to hit the metropolitan streets, *a paper straw.*

The way Mama described it, that straw was a marvel. And thanks to the growing popularity of soda fountains, they were all the rage with the wealthy and fabulous. The girls drank their Coca-Colas through the straw and felt as fine and fancy as anyone. Later, when they were nursing glasses of milk, they decided to innovate with a little invention of their own. There were scallions growing in the garden, so they picked a few, hollowed them out, and used the gutted tubes as makeshift straws. Onion milk must have tasted just as bad as it sounds, because for the rest of her life, Mama couldn't stand to eat onions in anything. She couldn't even bear the smell of them. Just the mere whiff of them cooking was enough to make her gag.

Despite growing up poor, Mama got a good education and excelled at her studies. By some miracle, we still have her report cards from Craven County Schools, yellowed, handwritten records of straight *A*'s and *B*'s all throughout her elementary and high school years. From what I can make out from the notes, her teachers absolutely adored her. She was kind and beautiful, and as diligent in her studies as she was in everything else she did.

The name at the top of her report card was always written as Adaline, never Lanie. According to Mama's stories, the kids on the bus made fun of her first name with all the oomph and imagination of typical elementary school bullies. They'd spend the whole ride chanting, "Lanie, Lanie, Lanie."

I know. Real original.

Not much bothered Mama, but that sure did. If there was one thing she was particular about, it was getting her name right. That incident was enough for her to go by Adaline for the rest of her life. "It's easy to remember," she would tell people. "Just add *a line*."

The schoolyard bullying must not have deterred her too much after that because she graduated as valedictorian of her high school class in 1945. The country was battling the Axis powers on dual fronts, goods were being canned, and as young men and women came back and forth from war, hearts were being broken across the land.

Mama had little to do with the heartbreaking, however. She recalled that in the fourth grade, a little boy named Samuel passed her a note and asked her to marry him. Mortified, she rushed home that day to show the note to her father. I guess nothing much came of it because there's no fourth-grade wedding on record. There are certain things, I suppose, that are just better left to fizzle out on their own—cow choirs and underage marriage proposals, in particular.

Her whole life, she felt guilty about not replying to Sam's note. Personally, I hope that young Samuel went on to recover from his elementary school heartbreak, but only time will tell. The ultimate irony is that many years later, when Mama was a widow, Helen offered to reintroduce the two in hopes they could spark some companionship. "No thank you," Mama told her. "I'm very content."

But that was Mama for you. She would *never* do anything wrong or even anything that could be perceived as a slight against someone else. I've spent a lot of time thinking about where this came from and how it manifested in her life. Even as an adult, she never blamed others for their anger or wrongdoings. She figured it was always something *she* must have done. Part of this was just her nature. Part of it must have been being raised a strict Freewill Baptist. But a bigger part of it, I think, was the home she was raised in.

My grandmother Lanie Hall had some spunk to her, but Mama's daddy, Frank, was nothing but patient and mild. He didn't drink, and despite the flavor of the times, he never raised a hand nor turned to a belt to discipline his children. His favorite Bible passage was Romans 5:3–5, particularly the part about tribulation producing patience.

Mama recalled the time when she and Helen sneaked behind the chicken house to try a cigarette. Their father, of course, caught them, but there was no shouting, threats, or even a punishment. My granddaddy simply looked at them and said, "Daddy's girls don't smoke."

That was something that imprinted on my mother, something she remembered the rest of her life. When she told the story, I could *feel* the guilt and the shame she carried. It wasn't about the cigarette, per se. It was more of the fact that she'd disappointed her father. She adored, looked up to, and respected that man to her dying day. He never needed to punish her. His approval or consternation was enough.

I'm awfully proud of how close my family is today, but I know for a fact my kids don't see me the way my mother saw her father, or even the way I saw Mama throughout my childhood. As I mentioned, I think a lot of this has to do with my parents' gentle natures—something that's passed down throughout our family, but apparently not to me.

I guess you can say that about the familial closeness too. Of course, Mama and her siblings were close. They were all one another had. Their church—and that little community of Dover, North Carolina—was all they had. In the 2010 census, that town only registered 401 people. Their town was tight-knit, and in the wake of the Depression followed soon after by World War II, they had to be.

That kind of hardship wasn't hardship in those days. It simply was what it was. And that kind of hardship can't help but breed closeness. Mama always spoke of Helen's engagement as the deepest sort of betrayal. The two were so close, she couldn't imagine having to share her older sister with anyone else. "You don't love me anymore," she told

Helen. And while that might have been a bit overdramatic, there's something real and raw that rings true.

Helen *couldn't* love Mama anymore—not in the way they'd grown up to love each other, anyway. Marriage meant no more cuddling with cold feet at night. Marriage meant no more singing in the bathroom or serenading dairy cows. Marriage meant that Helen was starting out with a life of her own, and the life that she'd known with Mama would never be the same. They would never again be as close as they once were, and I think there was a part of my mother that mourned that, even as an adult. Even when she grew old and moved down to a gorgeous condo on a sunny Florida beach, she could hardly stand to be away from her sisters.

It didn't take long for Mama to go off and get herself married, though. She was pretty, educated, and hardworking, and women like her didn't fail to get noticed.

It became a great center of debate in the family whether or not my parents ended up meeting at a weenie roast, but I went back to the records and confirmed that was a sidestep from the truth. My daddy, George Edward Gray, first laid eyes on her at Marston's Drug Store where she was working her first job. He was eighteen years old, and even though he didn't have any education past the eighth grade (he was too busy playing hooky and riding along on supply trucks), he was well on his way up the ranks of the Lance Cracker Company. His dad had sold fish and peanuts on a street corner, so the job was a leg up as far as the family fortune was concerned. His home wasn't religious, but my daddy never cursed. He had big-time morals, and everyone on his cracker route adored him.

I've since confirmed that the weenie roast at Gray's Mill was Mama and Daddy's first *date*. For the next two years, he went to the drugstore for lunch every day and asked her if she would marry him.

Well, golly, she thought to herself. *This poor man is asking me every day.*

"All right," she finally told him, "but you've got to ask my parents first."

She arranged for her cracker-peddling beau to come over for a visit. The whole time, she was waiting for him to pop the question, but Daddy never managed to pluck up the courage to do it. Apparently, he sat on the couch and didn't say a word. Mamma could talk to any stranger; she had personality coming out her ears. But George Gray was a shy, reserved man. He never did end up honoring her one request, and she remembered still being mad at him even when she agreed to marry him anyway.

My parents didn't talk much in terms of their young romance, but if there's one thing that sticks out in my mind, it's my daddy's gentleness. For some reason, he went by the name Pete (and sometimes Re-Pete) and even though he wasn't a churchgoing man, he had a kindness about him that I can't help but think reminded Mama of her own father. The Gray family owned a corn mill as well as a store, a dance hall, a pond, and even a zoo. But way back when, there was some sort of split (a typical family feud over who got this or who was responsible for that) that left them divided. The details are a little fuzzy, but from my memory, there was a relatively wealthy side of the family and a poor side of the family.

My daddy fell on the poor side of the Gray family, but that didn't mean he and Mama were unhappy. They ended up being married without the bells and whistles of a big wedding. They simply drove to Dillon, South Carolina, to the local courthouse. Mama would talk about standing there with a giant mirror behind them, waiting to sign the papers. Mama said Daddy always had a sloped head, and she would always bring this up in her stories as she aged. Mama remembers being in the courthouse and looking back at her own reflection, standing there with her sloped head guy, and thinking, *Adaline, what have you done?*

Whatever they did, they must have gotten something right. My parents were married on October 10, 1948, and they stayed married until Daddy's death in 1999.

In those fifty-one years, the biggest threat to their union were what my mom described to me as the "hoochie-coochie" girls, morally questionable women who would get gussied up and ride along with the county fairs. According to Mama, one of them had the audacity to sidle up to my daddy and ask him for a cigarette light. Mama was never one to get angry or defensive, but as the story goes, she wasted no time wedging herself between Daddy and the hoochie-coochie in question. He may have had a sloped head, but Mama wasn't about to leave any uncertainty about his romantic availability.

"He's *my* man," she said. "Get your own."

Mama may have been one of the sweetest, mild-mannered women to have ever graced this earth, but she didn't mess around when it came to wanton fair women. When people ask what the secret is to a long and happy marriage, I can't help but wonder if staking your claim in front of hoochie-coochie girls has something to do with it.

I *do* know, however, that my parents were happy wherever they were, even if that meant finding joy in having little. Not a lot of people can say that nowadays. Whatever Mama and Daddy did to keep themselves grounded in love, they were on to something—something we should probably take the time to learn for ourselves.

When we think about someone growing up in a different era, it's easy to dismiss their lives as "simpler" than our own. Sure, they didn't have a drone that delivered Amazon packages to their door. They planted, farmed, and canned their own food. But that food wasn't full of preservatives and chemicals either. To this day, I remember my grandma's cooking as some of the best I've ever eaten. They may not have had indoor plumbing or central heating, but that led to a different type of dependence—one that literally involved keeping one another warm through the coldest nights of winter.

To say our ancestors' lives were easier or even old-fashioned isn't just derivative, it's demeaning. It's subtly saying, in one way or another, that the lives they lived and the lessons they learned can't connect with our own, that these human experiences have no value in today's world.

The bits and pieces that I have of my mother's story show me that nothing could be further from the truth. Of course, things were different, but that doesn't mean those times have nothing to teach us.

I think about Mama recalling a good, old-fashioned funeral, where all the neighbors would come out to the dead person's house not only to grieve, but also to share an experience. The neighbors would file into the house, bearing platters of some sort of food, then swing by the casket to pay their respects and even touch the body. As crazy as that might seem to us, this was the ritual, the way the community came together to bond and honor the one who'd passed.

Something as simple as an "old-time" funeral shows me how much we've lost. How many of us even know our neighbors nowadays? How many of us truly connect with our community, participating in social rituals not out of obligation or for religious reasons, but because we truly and honestly want to share a little bit of what it means to be human?

Sure, you can say things were simpler back then. But maybe that's because our generation has a harder time with simple things. Nowadays, when my grandkids ask for something, I can have it delivered to my front porch in twenty-four hours' time. They'll never know the joy and anticipation of watching for their daddy at the end of the road, knowing he's coming home with their annual bottle of Coca-Cola. They'll never know the magic of singing to a dairy cow or drinking fresh milk through an onion straw.

The snapshots I have of Mama's childhood are scattered and hazy. They're worn by time and memory, and I'm not always sure where they fit or if I even have an inkling of their true value. But even though I'm missing so many puzzle pieces of her story, that doesn't mean I can't admire the little bits that I can make out. Every piece—every story, memory, and even the seemingly random details—are beautiful in their own right. These scattered bits have so much to teach us on their own, and when I begin to try to piece them together, it really doesn't matter if my efforts are successful or not. The bigger picture, whatever it may be, is always something worth looking at. There's always something to learn and reflect on, something that makes me laugh, cry, or even just take a moment to reflect on my own story.

There will also always be generational gaps in experience and understanding. But if we take a moment to learn what those gaps are, the difference might not be as deep as we think.

If you take anything at all from this book, I want it to be this: *Talk to the ones you love.* Take the time. Make the space. Extend an intentional invitation for them to share their stories. Believe me when I say there is priceless value in whatever you may end up with, even if those pieces seem random, vague, or downright hyperbolized. I've found that the funniest, most far-fetched stories connect us to our loved ones, even after death. Don't wait until you're wishing for more time to start making the effort.

I know I'm never going to get my hands on that time machine, and I've made my peace with that. It was never really about the time machine in the first place. My mother's past isn't some distant world or quaint, old-fashioned reality. There's no great chasm between her experience and my own.

I'll pass on the time travel (for now), but the things I do wish for are more pieces of my mother's past, more time to sit and spool through the threads of memory that connect her stories to my own. The more I learn about Adaline Gray, the more I realize that her life wasn't simpler, nor was it any more complicated. We're both mothers, daughters, wives, and grandmothers. We've both navigated the world through poverty and riches, war and peace, grounded in a love for our families that's been passed down through generations. And even though the picture of my mama's life might not be complete, the memory of her love is enough to make that image beautiful.

3

Something Called COVID-19

If it had all happened just a few years—maybe even a few months—later, we could have saved her. I'm *99.9 percent sure* we could have pulled her through had I known back then what I know now.

And that's where the guilt starts up: woulda, coulda, shoulda. "I woulda done this or that differently." "I coulda made things different." "I shoulda known this, that, or the other."

Believe me when I say, this is a dangerous game to play with an active mind. A merciless, exhausting game. It's kept me up at night for years playing the events of early 2020 through my head on repeat. I still have nightmares about those days, but I think that's pretty normal, all things considered. That's the basis for trauma. When something happens that's so life-shattering—so impactful, inexplicable, and strange—you can't make sense of it, your logical brain is going to keep recycling those memories on loop in hopes of cracking the code. Understanding. Doing *something* different to ensure that whatever bizarre, dangerous, or upsetting thing happened, you can take the necessary steps to ensure that kind of thing never happens again.

But that's the issue with COVID—and that's what makes not talking about our experiences an even bigger issue. Not only are we left on our own to wrestle with these experiences as individuals rather than a community, we're left searching for answers that don't exist.

Why did it happen this way and not that way? Why did we know this and not that? Would things have just changed if we'd only . . .

Like most things, I don't think the answers to these questions are black and white. However, that doesn't mean we shouldn't be asking. If anything, the ambiguity makes our shared stories all the more important. Maybe we'll never find a rhyme or reason behind our individual struggles throughout 2020, but at the very least, we'll know we're not alone.

It's truly heartbreaking to hear others' stories about losing loved ones to COVID in 2020. And if I've been cycling through wouldas, couldas, shouldas for years, I'm sure others who lost someone are wrestling with similar experiences. Not a day goes by when I don't reflect on the end of my mother's life, planning, rehashing, and tweaking every detail to hypothetical perfection. And while I know that grief is far from a linear process, I also think this pandemic backseat quarterbacking is part of my own healing. My brain gets *what* happened. It just hasn't caught up to *why*. Maybe it takes pushing those wouldas, couldas, shouldas to the brink of exhaustion before I'm finally able to let them go. Or maybe they'll be in the back of my mind, spinning on endless repeat, until the day I die.

There are so many things I would have done differently had I known what I do now. But I guess that's true of just about everything, and I'm willing to bet money I'm not the only one who feels this way. Nowadays, we see many more people—the elderly included—making full COVID recoveries. But back when this all started, we didn't even know exactly what the virus was, much less how to treat it. You would think this would allow me to give myself a smidgeon of grace for decisions I made in the moment, but it only makes me wonder. What if Mama had been exposed to COVID in 2022 instead of 2020? What if, in an ironic twist of fate, it wasn't *getting* the virus that killed her—it was *when* she got the virus?

It's wild, I know, and probably not completely logical. But these are the thoughts of an extreme planner's grief-fueled brain. These are the things I think about as I stare at my ceiling, trying to fall asleep. When you start playing these mind games, there's always a new *who, what, when, where*, and *why*.

The "where" part is easy enough. I remember exactly where we were when COVID first blipped across my mental radar. Of course, I'd heard mentions on the news, but none of it seemed real—not until late February, at least. The family was on vacation together, and as the grandkids were splashing around and plunging down waterslides at the pool, I got to talking with the young lifeguard standing duty. She mentioned hearing about one confirmed case in a nearby county and that quite a few international travelers had been forced to cancel their trips. The conversation didn't go much further. I remember thinking how nice it was that the hotels weren't busy—how unseasonably empty, quiet, and slow everything seemed. Part of me hoped the rumors would blow by like a bad allergy season. Maybe this new sickness would stay far enough away that we could worry about it when we got home.

That's the thing about tragedy, the scary, unpredictable things in life you can't control—things such as war, sickness, or even horrific accidents. You see them all the time on the news, and you *feel* bad about them. But thirty seconds later, you can turn the TV off, thankful that, whatever it is, it's not happening to *you*, which means you can safely forget it.

Over the next week, I quickly realized how wrong I was. This wasn't something you could just switch off. By the time our family got home from that vacation, the whole world was in an uproar. Every major news channel was blowing up, new precautions and restrictions were coming down on what seemed like a daily basis, and social media posts ping-ponged between celebrity attention grabs and apocalyptic pictures of gutted Walmart shelves. You knew things were serious when churches started locking their doors—*churches*. Having spent nearly my whole life in the Carolina Free Will Baptist Church (including many late nights when Mama forgot something or wanted to drop by for an impromptu prayer session), a locked church door was something I never thought I'd live to see.

Anxious, was the journal entry for March 13, 2020. *Coronavirus. Can't see Mama. Scary times.*

The advice coming down was not to visit elderly family members due to risk of exposure—and rightfully so. That meant quarantining for fourteen days after our vacation. Then lockdown started, and my daughter Lauren opted to bring her children to our house so they would have more space for homeschooling and spring break entertainment. As happy as Gregg and I were to have them, this meant another fourteen days before I could risk visiting Mama. That worried me. By 2020, she'd been battling Alzheimer's for years. Anyone who's been around someone suffering from Alzheimer's or dementia will tell you that one of the most unsettling, upsetting, and confusing things for a patient is a change in routine—who they see, what they do, and what goes on in their daily schedule. As terrifying and chaotic as COVID was for us, I couldn't even begin to imagine what the experience was like for her.

Thankfully, Mama's caretakers stayed on even after the outbreak. Years before COVID, we had Sarah, who was an expert at keeping Mama clean and well-dressed, and Sarah's sister, Regina, who was always so loving and affectionate. As time went by and Mama's overall condition worsened, we also brought on a third woman, Harriet, to help Sarah during her shifts. For the past eight years, these three had worked together as the perfect team.

Things had been good. Predictable even. Had the pandemic not hit . . .

Well. My imagination could run wild with the what-ifs.

Gregg and I have never lived through anything like this, I wrote. *Time to remember that God's in control and not think ahead.*

It's kind of funny to look back on that entry. To ask me not to think ahead is like asking a bird to breathe underwater.

Meanwhile, protective equipment was in short supply. I scrambled to make sure Mama's team had the proper equipment, gloves, masks—the whole PPE ensemble. By this time, this "thing called COVID" was everywhere. Videos of silent city streets and blue-suited essential workers felt almost apocalyptic, and I know I'm not the only one who wondered about divine judgment. For the first time since we'd moved to Florida, the beaches were completely empty. Homeowners couldn't even walk on their property, and the neighbors were all too eager to call the local police on anyone who tried. It was a strange mix of fear and paranoia, being so desperate for life to go back to the way it was but knowing deep inside that was never going to happen. At first, the whole thing had almost a "snow day" feel for the kids, but as days turned to weeks and weeks turned into months, we started considering what *years* might look like.

Everyone has their own lockdown story, and as we bring them together, I'm sure we'll get even more insight into how much 2020 changed the human experience. There are depths of courage and hardship that we still haven't wrapped our heads around, nurses suiting up to work, not knowing if they would return with the same disease that killed one of their patients, or the mental toll of a family crammed together in a tiny city apartment for months on end. Every experience was different; you can't lump them into sloppy categories of "better," "worse," "good," or "bad."

My journal entries from this time tended to be short and serious. *We're very tired. Not sleeping,* I wrote one day. Early in April, I recorded that over five hundred people had died in New York alone. Regina, Harriet, and Sarah would send me pictures of Mama, and as great as it was to see her, I got a pang in my chest every time I did. The power of touch—physical connection such as holding hands, cuddling, or simply sitting close—is something we don't talk about enough when it comes to the elderly. I missed hugging my mama, holding her in my arms while we sang her favorite hymns. I would drop by every day to visit her through her screen door, but it just wasn't the same. Nevertheless, I was trying my best to keep her safe since I'd been around my daughter and young grandkids, and the advice at the time was to stay away from the elderly or immunocompromised if you'd been with people outside of your household.

As February melted into one long Groundhog Day somewhere between March and April, we tried to settle into our "new normal"—whatever that was supposed to mean. Mama's caretakers came and went according to schedule, but they also had their own lives navigating exposure with their own family and friends. I would remind them to be careful with who they saw and interacted with, but you can't constantly monitor every facet of someone's life. Taking care of Mama was a full-time job, and there was no way I could do it without the team. We could follow guidelines, wear our masks, and social distance according to recommendations, but that didn't stop the fear. What if we missed something? What if we hadn't been careful enough? Was it reasonable to ask the staff not to go to church? Not to get their food at the grocery store? To keep their distance from their own families, knowing they were going to have to get close to Mama?

The what-ifs make me sick to my stomach. What if I'd been stricter? What if I *had* been in control of every single factor? What if I'd just listened to my gut from the very beginning, and what if we'd known everything we know now way back then?

In late April, Harriet called in sick with a cold. And soon after, Sarah asked her sister, Regina, to take her shifts for two weeks. Harriet wasn't running a fever, but she agreed she needed to get tested right away. This was back when it took between three and six days to get results. She told us that her initial test came back negative, but only later would we find out she'd failed to mention a key detail about the situation: her daughter, who lived in her house and had close contact with her, had already tested positive.

We didn't know this at the time, though. Part of me suspects Sarah might have known, but whether or not Regina was in on that information, she kept showing up for work. She would later come down with the virus. Her husband would be hospitalized and nearly die in intensive care. And I only contracted the virus after I finally caved and went into Mama's apartment to hold her.

At the time, I was doing my best with the information I had. But do I lie awake at night, wondering what might have happened if something—*anything*—had gone differently? If I'd asked more questions or been a little less trusting of what people told me?

You bet I do.

But like I said, this book isn't about the blame game. I don't truly know where things started and what happened behind the scenes, only which clues and timelines seem to add up. But at the beginning of the pandemic, we didn't even know what information to depend on. We were receiving conflicting messages about whether or not this disease lived for hours on exposed surfaces, if patients should or shouldn't be put on respirators, and how many masks you needed to layer to keep yourself safe. The world was playing a massive game of scientific catch-up, and the stakes were human lives. Sprinkle in a hefty dose of misinformation, fearmongering journalism, and nationwide panic, and the wouldas, couldas, shouldas add up fast.

Had I known what I know now about the pandemic, the situation, and Mama's condition, could I really have saved her? I'd like to think so. But that last little itch of doubt—that *measly .1 percent* of my 99.9 percent surety—is still there. To be honest, I'm not really sure which is worse, knowing there was something I could have done or my complete, unshakable surety that I was, in the end, utterly helpless to save her.

So my mind keeps rolling on repeat, replaying the situation in hopes of finding some sort of peace in all these questions. What if I woulda trusted my gut? Maybe I shoulda been stricter about knowing who Mama's caretakers had been exposed to. If there were some sort of magical do over, is there an ideal situation where I coulda saved her?

There's so much pain around these questions. It hurts on a family level, a community level—the hopeful, scrappy part of me that used to be so much more trusting. But in the swirl of grief, loss, and failure, there's also part of me that knows these answers won't take the pain away. The questions will always be there, a stain on my brain too deep to forget, but too faded for anyone else to remember. And maybe that's just a part of healing.

4

My Mother

It's impossible to get out of parenting unscathed. No matter what you do or how well you do it, your child is going to find something to criticize.

It took me growing up and having children of my own to truly understand this. I'll never forget when my father-in-law told me, "Your kids will never love you as much as you love them." At first, this sounded totally ridiculous. Growing up, I loved my parents more than anyone. I obeyed them. I admired and respected them just as much as the next dutiful daughter.

However, as I would soon learn after becoming a mother myself, there are different types of love, and even the strongest, purest love grows and changes over time. That's a hard thing to understand when you're young. As kids, the first formative thing most of us experience is the world our parents have constructed. Expectations are set, and behaviors are modeled for better or for worse. Some of us grow up with fantastic home lives, loving parents, and plenty of food in the pantry. Others don't. But no matter what kind of situation you were raised in, you were still *growing up*. You were still learning and maturing, trying to find your way in a brand-new world, and a lot of those experiences are shaped by your parents.

When I was raising my kids, it often felt like a "damned if I do, damned if I don't" situation. I wanted to be home with them, but I wanted them to learn independence. I wanted to meet their every need, but I didn't want to spoil them. I wanted to raise them with the same solid foundational values that have served me throughout my life, but I didn't want them growing up the same way I grew up. Even though I was raised in a loving, stable home, I still wanted to do things differently than my parents did.

It's a paradox; an undefined, ever-shifting balancing act. My childhood was wonderful, but there were still things I wanted to change for my own kids. And even if my parents had somehow magically managed to do everything "right" (I put that word in quotes for a reason), I'm sure I still would have found something to criticize. That's not their fault, and it doesn't necessarily mean they did anything wrong. But that doesn't make a child's criticism any easier to swallow.

The fact of the matter is, we're human. We'll never be perfect at anything, much less the rip-roaring misadventure that is parenting. And even if we were, by some miracle, able to escape without the bumps and bruises of hard experience, just because something was right for us doesn't make it right for our children. We're all individuals, and we're all learning to make it through the world in our own way.

You can't see that as a kid. You don't have the perspective. The problem with growing up is you have to have something to *grow up into*. You have to figure out how to change, how to become your own person. That process can be cruel and frustrating, but it's also necessary. If we don't grow up questioning, we never learn how to see things differently. There has to be a time of rebellion—of growing, changing, and venturing out to gain our own experience.

I know I'm more fortunate than most. I came from a safe, loving household with two kind parents. We didn't have a lot of money, but I never went hungry, and while my life has never been perfect, I can look back at a childhood filled with cherished memories. However, that doesn't mean there weren't times I felt angry, frustrated, or less-than. My mother was the picture of Christian perfection, and while I was never a troublemaker in any way, shape, or form, it's been a journey to reconcile Mama (or, at least, my perception of her) with my own experience as a mother. The ironic thing is, I was never mad at her for what she did. I was always frustrated by the things she *didn't do*, how she kept quiet, blindly trusted authority, and gave to others even when she had nothing left. If there was ever any such thing as "too good," Adaline Gray was the posterchild incarnate.

"Marsha is my best critic," she would say when I would rattle off a smart-alecky comment. Even when I was a teenager, she never hushed me up. She never seemed to get mad or show any of her hurt.

I do know my criticism hurt her, though. It had to. It's crazy to look back now that my own children are adults and think about the times I was frustrated with Mama. When I threw those harsh words at her, there had to have been instances when she excused herself and cried behind a closed door. I've done that quite a few times when my children have hurt me—more times than I care to count, anyway. As the saying goes, "They step on your toes when they're little and on your heart when they're older."

It's easy to criticize your parents, and in a strange way, it's necessary. It's this kind of criticism—even the frustration at the things they can't control—that spurs us on to become our own people. It's not fair, but no one ever said growing up was anything close to fair. I was told I would end up turning out like my mother, but deep inside, I've always known that I'll never be anything close. Sometimes, that realization comes with a pang of guilt; other times, I feel nothing but gratitude for what our differences taught me. My mother was a kind, agreeable, and trusting person, and the traits that made her so wonderful might very well be the traits that made her so vulnerable.

I realize now that no matter what my mother had been like or what she did or didn't do, there always would have been growing pains no matter where we were in our relationship. That's just a part of maturing, and for better or for worse, that experience never stops. You choose to emulate certain traits of your parents, and you choose to let go of others. I'd always thought I was nothing like Mama, but looking back, I realize that I took more from her than I ever left behind.

Maybe growing up with Mama wasn't about what she did right or wrong. Maybe it's more about perspective, living and developing compassion and understanding for the people who raised us. We can't help the parents we're born to, and no matter what kind of childhood we had, that's forever a part of our story. I didn't always understand Mama, but I always loved her. And I know for a fact that I wouldn't be the mother I am today had she not been a mother to me.

Like most things in Mama's life, her motherhood journey started out quietly. My brother, Eddie, was born on September 17, 1953, when she was twenty-five years old. I came along later, on February 13, 1957. She may have been heading up her own household on 1704 Carey Road, Kinston, but there were certain leaves Mama took straight from *her* mama's book.

How to be happy with little, for instance. As long as I could remember, my parents both worked full-time jobs that never made them rich. Daddy still ran a route selling Lance crackers, but by the time my brother and I were born, he'd graduated to having his own truck. I remember riding along with him in the summertime when Eddie and I were out of school, bouncing up and down (no seatbelts, of course) in the middle aisle of the truck while we munched on crackers. Daddy would always make a jab about us eating up all his profits, but he never stopped us from snacking either.

Mama got a job at the Carolina Telephone Company where she worked for thirty-three years and five months as a switchboard operator. A lot of times, she had the night shift, and I remember going with Daddy to pick her up at work. On those nights, he'd take us out for cheeseburgers, fries, and Pepsi-Colas. It was a treat, but nothing beat the sight of watching her walk down the steps of that telephone company late at night.

Some nights, I would lie awake in my bed, knowing I could simply pick up the phone and hear her voice on the other end of the line. However, I also knew how terrified she was about doing a single thing wrong—including taking personal time to shoot the breeze with her daughter. Her perfect attendance records at her job and at church attested to the fact that she never called in sick. Even when the car broke down, she ended up walking the six miles to work. If I ended up too sick to go to school, a neighbor would come by to keep an eye on me.

And this was just her professional life. Besides working full-time at the telephone company, she also cut hair in our living room, sewed clothes, and baked and decorated elaborate wedding cakes. To this day, I'm a complete snob about my baked goods. She would construct masterpieces using orange juice cans or whatever else she had lying around the house. Her baking always ensured I was the teachers' favorite.

She drank coffee all day. Not good, fancy coffee. Watery, runny coffee that was little more than percolated bean juice. Even so, there was no telling how she managed to get everything done. She would always say, "I was born tired and had a relapse." Many times, even when she wasn't on an operator shift, she would stay up late into the night finishing a sewing project or putting the final touches on a cake. My mama worked relentlessly—my kids have said they never saw her sit until she got sick at the end of her life—and she did everything at her own pace.

We were always poor, but I never felt trashy. If anything, Mama's kind heart and ingenuity made our financial situation more like a grand adventure. When I was young, I wanted a trampoline. At that stage in my life, it felt like *everyone else* had them, and I begged for one, even though I knew we didn't have the money.

As unreasonable as this was, my mama was the kind of woman who made lemonade with pretty much anything. She took an old box spring and mattress we were replacing and dragged it out into the yard, letting my brother and me jump on it until it completely fell apart from the combination of the rain and countless hours of joyful wear and tear. By the time we actually threw it away, there was wet cotton all over the yard.

Mama was always making something out of nothing. Still, I'll never forget how much I loved to visit other peoples' houses. Our house wasn't particularly nice or fancy, and I would go over to my playmates' and absolutely drool over how big the rooms were or how fancy the furniture looked.

After visits like that, I'd come home in a frenzy and rearrange the furniture in my room, trying to make it "work better"—whatever that meant. I did this for years, and at one point, I decided I liked my parents' bedroom better than my own. Sure enough, Mama and Daddy moved out of their room and let me move in, if only to make me happy. That's just the kind of people they were.

Sometimes, I look back and think to myself, *Would Gregg and I have moved out of our bedroom if one of our children arbitrarily decided they liked it better and wanted to play house with the furniture?*

Ha. That's a laugh.

But Mama had a way of making even the simplest things magical. She was always running herself ragged, trying to keep everyone happy and do good by all. Raising two rambunctious children while working a full-time job is more than enough for anyone, but her time volunteering at church should have counted as *another* full-time job on top of everything else. Some of my earliest, most consistent, and funniest memories all take place in the Free Will Baptist congregation. It didn't matter how young, sick, or tired we were—we were packing up and heading to service. If we were traveling, we would find a church along the way and pay a visit. A few times when I was too sick to make it, she had someone come out to the house and give the Sunday school lesson to me in bed so I didn't miss out. My brother, my mother, and I all ended up with dozens of perfect Sunday school attendance pins, and I would always joke with Mama about them getting me into heaven.

Every night when she was home, she would sit Eddie and me down for a Bible reading and prayer. Of course, we would be smart about it and choose the shortest verses such as "Jesus wept." But Mama would just sigh, shake her head, and then launch into one of her famous, gorgeously eloquent prayers that seemed to go on forever. Five, ten minutes . . . Eddie and I would finally open our eyes, catch each other's attention, and pretend to snore.

We weren't just Sunday church people. We were Sunday, Sunday night, Wednesday night, revivals, youth groups, holiday, Vacation Bible School, and any-other-day church people. Mama taught Sunday school, was in charge of every Christmas play, and even made most of the costumes. And my mother didn't just teach. She *preached*. She gave full-blown sermons about missions and would even be invited to go speak at other churches, which wasn't common for a woman at the time. Whatever money she had, she gave. And even if she didn't have money, she still gave. Our car became something of a church bus on Sundays. She would drive around and pick up all the kids who didn't have a ride or whose parents wouldn't take them. After the sermon, she would take us all out to ice cream—and I know she didn't have the money for that. When she finally did save enough to go on vacation, she opted to go on mission trips, first to Mexico and then to the Philippines.

"Others, Lord, yes others, let this my motto be . . ."

She knew every single word to every single song in the hymnal, but "Others, Lord, Yes Others" by Charles D. Meigs was always her favorite. I used to love standing beside her during service so I could look up and watch her sing.

One part of the Free Will Baptist Community that stands out starkly in my mind was the quarterly foot washing, a ceremony where the congregation would bring in tubs of water and wash one another's feet the way Jesus washed his disciples' feet. You would wrap a towel around your waist, bend down for the washing, and then trade places with the person in the chair.

None of the other children were required to attend, but you'd better believe Eddie and I were there. I was always self-conscious of my feet. A little girl had once pointed out how long and skinny my toes were, and I could never shake my self-consciousness about them. I started conning my best friend into going to church with me on foot-washing night so I didn't have to partner with an adult, but that just made for a spectacle. Throughout the whole ceremony, we couldn't stop giggling.

Mama, however, remained perfectly somber and serious. She kept her eyes reverently closed, and even though women would keep their panty hose on through the process, she would meticulously wash between every toe. While my best friend and I waited, exasperated and bored, for her to finish up so we could leave, she took all the time she needed to attend to the person in the chair. To her, it was more than foot washing. It was truly the reflection of something higher.

At the time, I was mortified that my mom spent so much effort washing someone else's feet. I didn't get it. I'm still not sure I fully understand now. But as I reflect on those ceremonies—the way she *made* them ceremonious by caring for every person—I see something different. Here was a woman who gave everything she had, including her time and attention, to make others feel special. To remind them through a simple action that they, too, were beloved children of God.

For as much time as we spent at church, my dad never joined us. You would think this would be a point of contention in their marriage, but Mama never spoke critically about him or demeaned him for it. My whole life, I always had a sense that my daddy was afraid to walk through those doors. When we would go to visit my grandparents on a Sunday and Mama would insist on pulling over to visit a church on the way, he would sit patiently in the car while we all went to Sunday school. My mama never pressed him. The church was such a key part of her life, but she never nagged him to take part in it. This was how it was for most of my childhood. Mama must have done an amazing job leading by quiet example because in the end, before my dad passed away, he did become a Christian.

For having such different churchgoing habits, my parents saw eye-to-eye on everything else that mattered. They never raised a finger against my brother and me or really even disciplined us. Their disappointment was always enough. Instead of telling me that I should or shouldn't do this or that, my parents would gracefully and quietly set an example.

As I mentioned, Daddy came from very gentle people, just like my mama. His daddy, who had started out running a horse and buggy, bartering peanuts and fish for chickens and eggs, eventually ended up running a little store between Sandhill and New Bern.

At that time, Kinston was segregated. One part of the street was for Blacks and the other was for whites. But that never mattered to Granddaddy. He opened his next venture, "Gray's Photos While You Wait," in what they called "Colored Town" and served anyone and everyone who walked through the doors. It was a tiny little shop with crazy signs, props, and backgrounds that he made himself. You could snap a silly picture with your friends and family, then wait while Granddaddy developed the photo right there on the spot. For the life of me, I don't remember what it cost (I seem to recall it was three for twenty-five cents), but I do remember that little shop being the place I fell in love with photography. My daddy would help his daddy every weekend, so I would spend my Saturdays there watching Granddaddy work or helping him develop pictures in the darkroom.

To my daddy and my granddaddy, it didn't matter what side of the street you were on. People in that part of town simply loved one another. There, in rural North Carolina, we were a community. My family ate at the Black-owned café next-door to the photoshop, and neither my parents nor my grandparents cared about the color of my playmates' skin. Considering the time and place, that was pretty remarkable.

My parents were kind people, just like their parents before them. They didn't fuss about much of anything—especially my mother. Back before Daddy met her, he'd had a girlfriend named Gaynelle who ironically ended up sitting behind us once when Mama took Eddie and me to see a Bozo the Clown show. We were sitting there in the audience, minding our own business, when Gaynelle poured her entire drink down Mama's back.

"You may have him now," she told Mama, obviously talking about my daddy. "But you won't keep him."

Mama didn't flinch. She didn't rile, react, or even turn around. When I think about that story today, my blood still boils. I know what *I* would have said to Gaynelle had I been old enough to use the proper words to express my true feelings. But Mama was unflappable.

Her saintly kindness was one of the reasons she was so adored, but I'd be lying if I said it didn't frustrate me as well. I'll never forget the time a young man who was interested in me showed up to our front door. He was truly a nice guy, and Mama liked him, which meant (in typical teenager fashion) I absolutely under no circumstance would want to keep seeing him. As soon as I saw him walking up to the door, I begged Mama to answer it and tell him I wasn't home.

"But, Marsha," she said, her face falling, "that's a lie. And lying's a sin."

I had to think quickly. "Fine," I said, "but what if I'm not *in the house*? Then saying I'm not home wouldn't exactly be lying, would it?"

So there I was crawling out the back window as Mama cheerfully went to answer the front door. I didn't have to deal with the poor guy, and her conscience stayed clear.

Unlike my mother, I wouldn't have lost a wink of sleep telling a little white lie to get rid of an unwanted caller. I was born with my Grandma Lanie's spunk. If something's wrong, I speak up about it, and if someone does wrong to me or one of my loved ones, you'd better bet I'm not going to keep my mouth shut. The part of my mother that could always turn the other cheek was a part of her I'll never fully understand. As wonderful as it was to watch her do good, it was horrible to watch other people take advantage of her.

Whenever there was a sick person who needed caring for, a baby being born, or a wound that needed dressing, sure enough, my mama was the one doing it. She never complained, and if I needed her after a long day at work, she never denied me her attention, even when she was dead tired. She often worked overtime so that Eddie and I could have things like other children at school.

She never questioned authority either. Doctors, preachers, teachers . . . in her mind, if God had put them in that place of authority, then they very well were meant to be there. If the preacher called a prayer meeting, it was time to pray. If the doctor gave her instructions, she followed them to a T. She took whatever came out of other peoples' mouths as gospel. And, of course, we can interpret this as naïveté, but my mother wasn't a stupid woman. She wasn't hopelessly gullible; she *chose* to believe in others' goodness, even when that ended up getting her hurt.

Still, it was a beautiful thing to know my mother cared so much about everyone. Every night after church, she'd give rides home to those who couldn't drive themselves, including a man named Hulon who lived in a group home. I remember Eddie and me sitting in the backseat, exhausted after a full day of school and hours of homework left undone, pointedly clearing our throats as Hulon chatted up Mama for what felt like hours. But she would never interrupt him, never cut him off. For Mama, it was more than just offering a ride. She truly gave with all her heart, her time, her energy, and her attention.

Never in my life have I seen anyone embody Jesus's teachings the way my mother did. If someone was sick, she cared for them. If someone was poor or needed help, she was the first one to give. Even when a woman in our community was infamously convicted of murdering two husbands and a two-year-old child, Mama went to visit that woman in prison, even when the rest of the community had (understandably) turned their backs on her.

All throughout my childhood, our front door might as well have been revolving, open to anyone at any hour. Mama always welcomed them and somehow always managed to feed them. No matter how poor we were, scrounging up food for drop-in guests was never a problem. She was the kind of woman who never failed to come up with something, the kind of woman who could feed a multitude with loaves and a few fishes. People even got married in our house, saying their vows right there in the living room.

She was never stingy, and she never treated hospitality as anything other than a joy. Someone could drop in at the most inconvenient time, and she wouldn't hesitate to welcome them. They even called her on the phone at all hours of the day, seeking a solution or even just a listening ear. I remember that phone, hung up high on the wall with the cord dangling down to the floor. Thankfully, the line was long enough to stretch through half the house. Mama would be on the phone for hours, doing housework or whatever else she needed to while lending her time and attention.

My mother embodied the Christian ideal of having a servant's heart, and part of me resented that. Well, that's not quite right. It wasn't resentment as much as it was a deep longing. When she was driving around to pick up a gaggle of Sunday school kids or serving as a caretaker for other people in the congregation, I seethed with jealousy, especially into my teenage years. *I* wanted that time with my mother, and even though she never denied me her affection, it burned me up to see her giving so much to other people—especially when they gave nothing in return or downright took advantage of her.

Unlike Mama, I get skeptical, especially when it comes to other people's intentions. Shrewd distrust is a part of my nature, but it has also come about from hard experience. Even as a grown woman, I saw people abusing Mama's kindness left and right. Of course, I'd tell her so, but she would just smile and shrug. While it infuriated me, it also made me feel responsible. I got the sense that, somehow, I had to protect her.

When I was a teenager, there was a woman down the road who suffered from severe anxiety. She would have intense episodes and end up calling my mother to come over and help her, but the instances became so long and so frequent, I ended up writing to her children to get their mother professional help. "My mom can't do everything," I told them, even though I very well knew if I didn't intervene, Mama would have *happily* done everything.

And that was the frustrating part. I couldn't be angry at her for being *too* helpful or *too* kind. That's just who she was. "I love people, and I love the Lord," she would say. "That's all I am." And she modeled that in everything she did, even when it came at her own detriment.

It's easy to backseat quarterback my mother's life and criticize her for not taking care of herself. But I'm sure my kids could accuse me of the same thing just as easily as they could fault me for not giving as freely as Mama did. It's a hard line to toe, and where you stand depends completely on what side you're looking from.

The fact is, I'll never be the woman my mother was. For a long time, that made me feel like a bad person, but now that I've grown up a little, I see that it's not a question of good or bad, right or wrong. There's no need for criticism or judgment. We're different people with different lives, raising different children in completely different situations.

My whole life, I swore I would feed my family on nothing but beanie weenies before I became a working mom. That's not because I resented Mama for working so hard, and that's not an indictment of any fantastic, hardworking mother who juggles her family life with a professional career. I was so adamant about staying home with my kids because, growing up, I yearned for my mother. She was always giving so much to so many. Part of that is my own jealousy, and that's not easy to reconcile.

Mama was an amazing woman, a staple in our community and a mother to so many people who needed that love and attention. I'm incredibly proud of her for that; I'm also incredibly selfish about my time with my own kids. My mother wasn't wrong for sacrificing so much of herself for others, but I've also had to reconcile that Mama and I aren't the same person. My choosing to stay home with my children (and having the luxury to do so) didn't make her wrong any more than volunteering to sew the costumes for the annual church pageant made her right. She was a good person—"too good," if there ever were such a thing. But that by no means makes me a bad one.

Of course, Mama worked herself to the bone. She was born into a house without indoor plumbing at the onset of the Great Depression. Of course, she trusted everyone around her. She was a woman of great faith who came from a tight-knit community. But looking back, I can also see how Mama's giving so much left her no time to take care of herself. It's a double-edged sword, neither right nor wrong, naive nor noble.

Jesus told his followers to turn the other cheek, but in the book of Matthew, he also warned them to be "shrewd as snakes and innocent as doves." It's hard not to see those passages as a paradox. Being selfless does make you vulnerable, and overworking inevitably takes a toll. But if doing a good thing ends up being bad for you, does that make it a bad thing? And if looking out for your own interests ends up strengthening you and your family, is that still selfishness?

These days, I see much more of a "me generation," and that's not necessarily a bad thing. People are taking time and talking about self-care. Workers are speaking out about the spiritual and emotional toll of the corporate hamster wheel and how it's damaged us as a society. There're societal skepticism, protests, conspiracy theories . . . Certainly, we've seen how mistrusting authority can lead to devastating consequences. But we can also see that the other end of the spectrum—blind trust and obedience—can be just as dangerous.

Maybe generational differences aren't meant to divide us. Maybe they're meant to *teach us*. When we choose to do things differently from our parents, that doesn't have to come from a place of judgement or regret. We can simply acknowledge that we're different people living different lives in completely different circumstances. I can sit here and criticize my mother for giving too much, but her selfless spirit is the same reason hundreds of loving cards, photos, and letters came flooding in after her death.

I'm sure my kids have plenty of criticism about my parenting. But that critical thinking, everything they want to do differently in their own lives, is an important part of growing up. And until we figure out a way to perfectly exist in the balance between trust and skepticism, giving and receiving, serpents and doves—no parent will ever escape unscathed.

5

The Fight for Breath

We all know we're going to die. It's an uncomfortable fact, but a fact all the same. I keep bringing it up because I know how easy it is to ignore this nasty little truth. When the topic does come up (and believe me, it will—often in the most unlikely circumstances), it can be a comfort to know there are plenty of resources and rosy images to help you swallow the bitter pill of mortality.

Of course we're going to die. But we imagine ourselves dying in a big, comfy bed, surrounded by friends and family laughing and crying over all the wonderful memories we've shared. We imagine there'll be some sort of hospice service, nurses and doctors who will guide us in peace and comfort to the great beyond. We have the technology. We have the medicine. Dying, in theory, should be a relatively simple, straightforward ordeal.

Let's not miss the key word there—*should*. It's one thing to make plans, even when it comes to aging and death, but we *also* know that the best-laid plans are the first ones to fall apart. When Mama received a positive COVID test at the age of ninety-one, I knew all my careful planning—the money and the years of preventative, holistic care—weren't going to count for anything. This global pandemic was a whole new ballgame, and it seemed like the rules were constantly changing.

The trouble started long before we got any positive tests, though. I remember going down to Mama's tiny apartment and talking to her through the screen door all throughout the first part of lockdown. It was more than the obligatory six-foot distance, but it might as well have been miles away. She would watch me, beg me to come in and see her, but I was too afraid.

As quarantine steadily metamorphosed from a temporary measure to a new reality for our foreseeable future, Mama stopped wanting to eat. This, we knew, was typical of Alzheimer's patients. Our family doctor assured me that as long as we got her so many meal replacement shakes a day, she would be fine.

But then I started getting more concerning messages from the caretakers. She was weakening, but it wasn't just because she was eating less. "She's giving up," they kept telling me.

I didn't believe it, but maybe that was because I didn't want to.

As I mentioned earlier, my daughter Lauren and her family came to hunker down with us during the lockdown, and as was advised, I waited fourteen days to go see Mama. When she spotted me outside, she beckoned, her voice frail and raspy. "Come here."

Tears sprang to my eyes. Everything crashed down at once. The guilt. The regret. The pain and confusion of not knowing what to do. I didn't want to put my mother in any danger. But she was *calling* to me.

"Mama," I told her, my voice catching in a choke, "I can't. I'm not supposed to . . ."

When I visited the next day, I couldn't stand it any longer. In full protective gear, I went into that little apartment and held her in my arms. This must have been when I contracted COVID myself, but looking back, I don't regret it. It wasn't about what was right or wrong. I could drive myself crazy thinking about everything that could have been. What happened, happened.

But even that day, I knew something was amiss. I'd seen Mama frail and weak, but this time, she was a ghost of herself. Even when I offered her favorite drink, her beloved Pepsi-Cola, she spat it straight out. And anyone who knew my mama knew that was something she'd *never* do.

That day, I asked her a question I'd posed countless times over the last few years. "Mama, do you want to see Jesus, or do you want to live?"

It must have taken all her energy to summon up a single word: "Both."

I went home sobbing. There was something seriously wrong—wrong beyond what I'd seen of her these last few years. I called our family doctor to order her a chest X-ray, and they said they would have the results by midnight. We waited and waited, and that Friday, it came back that Mama had double pneumonia and a broken rib. COVID, of course, was on the back of my mind. All things considering, pneumonia seemed like the best-case scenario.

"We'll get her a pill," the doctor assured me.

"No, you don't understand," I said. "She's not eating or drinking. How am I going to get a pill in her? We need intravenous antibiotics."

"I'm more concerned about her not eating," he said.

"Well," I shot back, "don't you think it'll be easier for her to eat when she has medicine and fluids to fight the pneumonia?"

We argued back and forth until he agreed to order the liquid medicine. But when I went to the pharmacy to pick it up, sure enough, the antibiotic was in pill form. It took hours for us to get in contact with him and reorder the medicine as a liquid. By the time we got back to Mama's apartment to give it to her, she was even worse. Even in liquid form, she couldn't get anything down. We nearly choked her trying.

"She needs fluids," I told the doctor.

"You need to take her to the ER," he shot back.

This wasn't the answer I was looking for. I'd seen the news. My daughter Brittany, a certified physician assistant, was clear about what would happen if it came down to hospitalization. For the elderly, the ER was just as good as a death sentence. The seniors who went in didn't come out, and family wasn't allowed to stay with them throughout the process.

"If you take Grandma to the emergency room," Brittany told me, "you may never see her again."

There was clearly a triaging system, and everyone seemed strangely calm about that. No one openly proclaimed the pecking order of human worth, but the sentiment was clear by the way seniors were treated. *What happens to them doesn't matter. They've had their time. They're going to die anyway.*

It's a chilling thought, but the attitude goes much deeper than the things we don't say out loud. Look who's valued in our society. Look who graces our billboards, our screens, and our glossy magazine covers. Our generation doesn't value the old the way we do the young. We see our elderly as eyesores, as burdens and unwanted responsibilities. But as the average lifespan increases, along with longevity and medical technology, we can't escape the fact that we're making our own beds—quite literally. When we devalue the elderly, when we see them as less-than and disposable, we're setting the standard of how, one day, we ourselves will be treated.

Before we'd even heard of COVID, I'd seen firsthand how the hospital triage system treated senior citizens. Hospitals can't refuse anyone lifesaving care, but they can farm out patients—especially elderly patients—who don't have enough insurance coverage. When my father was desperately ill and close to dying, my brother walked into the rehab center to find him slumped over double in his wheelchair so far his head nearly touched the floor. He wasn't ready to begin the rehab process. He was barely conscious. He couldn't even hold himself upright.

When Mama was hospitalized back in 2015 with another case of double pneumonia and a broken back, she was in excruciating pain. It was the weekend of my husband's sixtieth birthday, so I was scooting back and forth from the hospital to a houseful of guests. I ended up skipping the birthday party to be with Mama. The doctor was giving her as much pain medication as she could physically tolerate. But Mama was still in agony. I'd never seen her in that much pain. She was pitiful. Here was a woman who'd never asked for help, who got up at three in the morning to shower when sharing a hotel room with my daughter so as not to inconvenience her. She was begging me to do something, pleading for me not to leave her alone. When the doctors finally treated her pneumonia, they wasted no time arranging for Mama to be transferred to a rehabilitation facility.

"There is no way I'm sending her to rehab," I told him. It took all I had not to shout. "How can she even *go* to rehab? How could she even start the rehab process with physical therapists when she has a broken back and is still in this much pain?"

The doctors went back in to operate on Mama's back, injecting bone cement into her fractured vertebrae to stabilize her spine. All the while, I couldn't get over the image of my father, slumped over and half-conscious, in the last rehab facility.

But that's the way the triage system works. When the elderly can't pay, you throw them away. It comes down to bed space. Money. And if elderly patients take up too much time in the hospital, you can always send them off to a rehab facility—whether they're ready or even capable of rehabbing in the first place.

All these experiences were on the forefront of my mind in 2020. Taking Mama to the ER was not an option.

"She needs intravenous antibiotics," I told the doctor. "We need to get her fluids."

I wanted to take her somewhere—anywhere but the ER. My husband and I had donated quite a bit of money to a local hospital wing, preempting that Mama would get bad and we would need a place to care for her. But that wing, the doctor told me, was closed due to the virus.

"We don't even have any blood work on her for me to be able to prescribe anything," he said—a little hiccup he'd failed to mention before.

Again, this was *not* what I wanted to hear. We argued back and forth and even hung up on each other at one point. He finally called me back, and his first words were, "Marsha, what do you want?"

"I want home health care," I told him.

There was a brief pause on the other end of the line. "I don't know if I can do that. It's a Friday."

Great, I thought. *If only Mama had chosen a "convenient" day to be on her deathbed.*

I was shaking when I finally got off the line. I sat there, trembling with fear and frustration, not knowing if he was going to call an agency or get us what we needed. I thought he ordered intravenous antibiotics, but as I very recently learned, he actually only ordered fluids. My mama never got any antibiotics except one liquid dose that she nearly choked to death on! Of course, I know they may not have helped since she had a virus, but we didn't know that at the time. At the time, all we knew was that she had double pneumonia.

This wasn't happening. It *couldn't* be happening. We'd made such careful plans, but in Mama's hour of need, all I could do was sit back and watch them unravel.

Relief came from a surprising place. After calling around frantically, trying to get Mama what she needed and seeing if anyone would come help her, an agency finally called me back that evening.

"You're so lucky," the woman told me. "We can send a guy over. We can't get the fluids until tomorrow, but he can come take a look at her."

This "guy" ended up being one of the true heroes, a nurse named Javier. I'm fully convinced this man is no less than an angel. When we talk about extraordinary essential workers, Javier is the first face that comes to mind. When the agency rang him, it was actually his day off. His family was in town, and he had big weekend plans to spend time with them. But he ended up coming to help anyway.

"Her vitals are pretty good," he told us. "I'll bring needles and start administering the IV fluids in the morning."

A blast of ice-cold fear rushed through me. *The needles.* I'd completely forgotten. The last time we'd taken Mama to the hospital for blood work, they'd stuck her four times with no success, leaving her utterly terrified and bruised black and blue.

*Frank and Lanie Hall,
Adaline's Parents*

*Adaline always
Loved School*

Behind the Barn

Beloved Sisters,
Helen and Adaline

Valedictorian, Dover High School

Sweet Adaline

*Lifetime Love
of the Beach*

Beautiful Inside and Out

Pete Gray, the Sailor

*Pete and Adaline,
at the Photo Shop*

Mama, Marsha, and Eddie

Mama's Baby Girl

Mama and Marsha

Adaline, the Family Hairdresser

*Daddy (Pete),
Marsha, and Eddie
at the Photo Shop*

Grandaddy Gray,
the Peanut Man

Grandaddy Gray at
His Photo Shop

Always Happy,
Always Smiling

The Gray Family: Pete, Adaline, Eddie, and Marsha

The Gray Family at Grandmama Lanie's Farm

Pete Gray, the Lance Man

Carolina Telephone Company Operator, Thirty-three Years

First Free Will Baptist Church
314 West Lenoir Avenue
Kinston, North Carolina 28501

The Church We Grew Up In

Perfect Attendance
Sunday School Pins

Mama's Church Children

Cragmont Assembly, Free Will Baptist Camp for Kids

*Missions Trip
to Mexico*

Missions Trip to the Philippines

Marsha, Mt. Olive College Cheerleader

*Gregg, Mt. Olive
College Basketball*

*Pickle Queen,
Mt. Olive College*

Mt. Olive College, Where It All Began

Mama Made Our Amazing Wedding Cake

Mama Was So Creative with All Her Cakes

Lauren's Birthday Cake that Mama Made

All the February Birthdays

"Don't you worry," Javier assured me. "I'm a trained pediatric nurse. I'll bring the tiniest needles you've ever seen."

That's when I burst into tears. After fighting with the doctor all day long, here was this person—this random man—who actually cared. He didn't just see my mama as a number or the next inevitable COVID fatality. He didn't know her as I knew her, the beautiful, caring woman who'd been a mother to so many. But he chose to value her. He chose to see her as a human life.

Javier didn't have to do what he did. He didn't have to go above and beyond his duties with such love, compassion, and understanding. But when we talk about heroes, he's someone we need to be talking about. People who not only stayed and held the line to do their jobs but did so *heroically* with heart and with courage.

He had no problem starting the IV, and for a while, her vitals were decent. For a brief moment—the faintest glimmer of a second—I had hope.

Maybe she doesn't have COVID, I thought. *Maybe it is just pneumonia.*

We'd fought and beaten pneumonia before. We could do it again. Maybe this wasn't the end. Maybe we could get through this. Maybe Mama's last days could be how I'd envisioned them, cozy and comfortable, surrounded by everyone who loved her.

The next day, Javier reported Mama had bed sores—something she'd never had before. My daughter Brittany noticed skin changes on Mama's feet. She texted a picture of her feet to her very good friend who happens to be a dermatologist at Stanford. Her friend wrote back, "Oh, no—COVID toes." Javier wanted Mama sitting up, but she couldn't even keep herself upright. At that point, he wasn't even supposed to be at work, but he chose to stay throughout the weekend.

Mama's vitals started worsening. Brittany and I were frantically calling anywhere and everywhere we could to try and get oxygen, but no one would deliver without a doctor's orders, and it was even more complicated to coordinate anything over the weekend. Finally, Monday afternoon, after watching Mama gasping for three days, we got the machine delivered, and Javier wasted no time getting Mama settled. I called a pulmonologist friend in Cocoa Beach who agreed to make an assessment over FaceTime video. After the first call, he told us to increase the oxygen and give it another day. But after the second, he recommended we start making hospice arrangements.

Many people don't know that hospice isn't like a hospital. It's not an instantaneous check-in, check-out process. You have to contact them ahead and make detailed arrangements. Our family doctor told me he'd already contacted hospice, but when we made the call to the facility, we learned that he'd done no such thing. Brittany started calling the facilities he claimed to have contacted, only to learn that those preliminary calls had never been made.

By May 3, Mama's vitals were showing signs of things getting dangerous. She couldn't even hold up her own head. That was the point I knew beyond the shadow of a doubt that she wasn't just sick—she was dying. This wasn't about getting her better. This was about making her as comfortable as possible until the end of everything.

I just didn't understand. After all my careful planning, there had to be something, *anything* I could do to keep her comfortable as things got worse. I wasn't hearing back from hospice. I wasn't ready to take her to the ER, knowing she would die there alone. The triage system, with its cold logic and statistics, would say that this was ridiculous, that I was wasting my time delaying what I knew was going to happen anyway. But I couldn't live with the idea of Mama suffocating. I couldn't stomach the thought of her spending her final moments gasping for air when there was something I could do.

When our doctor finally surfaced that Sunday after radio silence—not even showing up to *his* scheduled meetings—everything came to a head.

"How's Mama?" he asked.

I'll be the first to confess, that was the point I lost my temper.

"How's Mama?" I shot back, exasperated, practically spluttering. "*How's Mama?* You've been MIA for days. You haven't been there. You didn't contact hospice like you said you did, and you won't return our calls. I've been begging for oxygen—for *anything*."

The line went quiet for a moment. "Shame on you, Marsha," was all he said. Then he hung up.

We never spoke again.

I shouldn't have blown up. I know that full well. But at that point, I could hardly stand to look at my mother.

Every time I closed my eyes, all I could see was her lying there, struggling for every rasping breath. And all I could do was sit there and watch.

Of course, there was morphine. Of course, we could have said goodbye to her at the doors of the ER. But this wasn't the comfortable, loving scene I'd envisioned for the end of my mother's life. There were no adoring friends, no laughing, weeping family members praying over her and holding her hands.

I know I shouldn't have shouted at that doctor. But there was so much rage, so much grief, fear, and helplessness.

This wasn't the way things were supposed to go.

Even with Javier on our side, every step in the process felt like a downright skirmish. Mama lay in bed, wheezing, as we fielded phone calls at one hundred miles per hour. By this time, the news has spread. My brother, Eddie, Mama's sisters, all my children and grandchildren . . . everyone wanted to know what was going on and what was being done. Of course, I also had COVID, but I was running on sheer adrenaline. My stomach was a mess, and my body was ready to collapse beneath me—but I didn't stop. Even if I'd wanted to stop, I don't think I would have known how.

All the while, I kept thinking about the struggle. The struggle to breathe. The struggle to know what to do. The struggle to get Mama what she needed or even to get someone on the phone. No amount of time, money, or preparation could have helped that. Nothing I'd done had saved me from having to fight tooth and nail for my mama's last moments.

Looking back on all this chaos, I can't help but wonder if, someday, someone is going to fight for me. Will they be willing to yell at a doctor? Willing to spend hours on the phone juggling conflicting information to make sure I'm comfortable in my last days? How far will my loved ones be willing to go to make sure I can breathe? That my death, after all I've seen and done, is a *good* death?

When most of us envision passing on, we envision something peaceful, something quiet and reverent in the company of the ones who loved us most. But most death isn't peaceful. It's a struggle, a fight for dignity all the way to the bitter end.

The truth is, we triage seniors because things are just easier that way. Not everyone has the money. Not everyone has the time, the power, and the resources to fight for a dying loved one. And even with all those things combined, our medical system was ready to do with my mother what it does with countless others—toss them away and wait for them to expire. It's a grim reality. No wonder so many of us are terrified of aging.

The irony of throwing away seniors, of taking away the honor, grace, and dignity of a life's end, is that we make death something to be feared. Death can be scary, for sure, but each person should be given the ability to die with peace and dignity, and each life should be honored.

6

My Teacher

I didn't realize how much Mama was there until she was gone. Losing a parent is ironic that way. You never know what you have until you're looking at the empty space left behind.

It's only natural for kids to grow up preoccupied with their own lives. The Bible is pretty clear about a child leaving their mother and father in order to start a family of their own. It's a strange thing, spending eighteen-plus years living and learning in someone else's world, only to break off and start forging a path for yourself. Independence is a huge step for a child; it's also a major change for the parents.

Most all of us end up leaving the people who raised us, but that doesn't necessarily mean we leave them behind. The ghost of our upbringing will always be there, and for many of us, our parents take on completely different roles in our lives—mentors, counselors, grandparents, and even friends. As I set out to blaze my own trail, Mama was all these things and more. She was always supporting me, even in the times where I was too overworked and overwhelmed to see her. Motherhood was a major milestone in my life, and I was so busy adapting to my own rapidly shifting roles, I didn't take the time to appreciate how she seamlessly shifted into hers.

When you're young, you don't understand transition the same way. It's not a fault or a shortcoming; it's just the natural way of life. I became a mother very quickly, and I had five children in six years. Believe me when I say that *nothing* prepares you for that. All of a sudden, I was a grown-up. I had my hands full trying to take care of my young family, and that didn't give me much time to think about my mom and dad. It always registered that they were my parents and that I loved them, but my view of their lives was filtered through the lens of my own experience.

Even when we're grown, we often find ourselves depending on our parents. It's a natural state of order. Of course, it doesn't always happen this way, but as my kids have grown up and had kids of their own, I've come to understand the cycle a bit more. You want your kids to grow up to be strong, resourceful, and independent. You don't want to helicopter, infantilize, or hold them back from their true potential. However, that doesn't make it any easier to accept when your children don't need you in the same way they used to—when they blast out of your world and expect you to shift your orbit into theirs.

Seeing your children grow into their own is a joy-ous transition, but a transition all the same. And, like all transitions, there are growing pains. Family roles change, and so do expectations. I would be lying if I said my journey from mother to empty nester to first on the babysitting roster wasn't an adjustment. There's no magic light switch that flips in your head when you have a baby. Or when your baby has a baby, for that matter.

I've never seen anyone in my life navigate that transition as lovingly and gracefully as Mama did. Looking back, I realize what a staple she was not just as a physical presence, but also as a mentor and teacher for me and my kids. I don't think I appreciated it at the time because I couldn't have possibly imagined life without her, nor did I truly understand what it meant to navigate the trials and triumphs of grandparenting. But now that Mama's gone, I can finally see the gaping spaces she used to fill. And as much as it aches to miss those empty places, I'm also overwhelmed with love and gratitude.

I learned so much in Mama's presence, and in her absence, she teaches me even more about what it means to find the beauty in every season of life. These days, I'm a grandmother to fifteen beautiful grandbabies. Of course, my kids still depend on me. They're building lives for their families, and I'm thankful I have a place in those lives. I can be a part of something bigger, and while my life may look different than it did with young children, the role of the loving supporter overflows with its own kind of indescribable joy. I'll never be the grandmother Mama was to me and my kids, but I know I wouldn't be the grandmother I am today had she not been there for me. She was kind.

Compassionate. Unshakable and open-minded. And while I know we're two very different people, I also know that the way she lived back then has shaped the way I'm present for my own family.

Sometimes, you don't know what you have until you lose it. But now that I can look back and reflect on Mama's life, I see how much she still teaches me every day—how a patient, quiet presence can be the most powerful leadership of all.

Believe me, it's not easy growing up with a saint for a mother. Adaline Gray wouldn't lie or curse. If you got mad at her or made a snarky comment under your breath, *she* would be the one feverously whispering prayers, begging for forgiveness. Many times, I found myself wishing she would do something wrong just so I could see her as a normal human being.

I was anxious, driven, and skeptical by nature, but Mama wasn't afraid of anything. She would take my brother and me to the church late at night when everything was pitch-dark. This was back when the doors stayed unlocked, when anyone could waltz in at any time and be hiding in the pews somewhere with you. Sitting there in the silence terrified me, but she wouldn't be swayed when she got it in her mind to go for a late-night prayer vigil.

"Why worry when you can pray?" she'd ask, the telltale lead-in to one of her all-time favorite hymns.

That was her motto, her mantra, her song. Decades later, she had to be rushed to the hospital where we found out she had colon cancer. They had kept her there for immediate, life-saving surgery, and the nurses came in to offer her drugs to help her stay calm.

"Why would I need something to calm me down?" she asked, a giant smile plastered from ear to ear. "Why worry when you can pray?"

And then she started singing, *"Why worry when you can pray? Why worry when you can pray . . . ?"*

At that point, *I* was the one who needed sedative drugs. Why worry? Because there are plenty of things to worry about. Like I said, I'm a planner who has my Christmas stockings stuffed and ready by the end of July. Worrying—anticipating the next thing that's going to happen and planning ahead—is a key part of how I function. I've always had to have a plan and know my next move. Of course, I trust that God's going to take care of me. But that doesn't mean I'm about to open a candle shop without a fire extinguisher.

Sure, Mama never worried. But Mama never worrying made *me* worry about her not worrying.

To put things simply, she and I were cut from different cloth. Different times, different people. But as I grew up and started making my own decisions, she never shamed me or demeaned me for them. Of course, I felt *incredibly* guilty when I sneaked out to get my ears pierced behind her back, but the guilt never was about the earrings. Her disappointment was like a boulder on my chest.

Body piercings aside, Mama always supported me in everything I did, even when it came time for me to come into my own. In the third grade, we moved out to the country (Daddy wasn't a fan of in-town taxes), and I had to take the bus to LaGrange School. I absolutely hated it. There was a girl there who bullied me every day. We heard the Baptist church was building a new school close to where we lived, so Mama promised, somehow, she would find a way to send me. It was a big sacrifice, but by hook or by crook, my parents scrounged up the money. I ended up going to the new school when it opened three years later and was a cheerleader through the eleventh grade.

This only matters because it's where I first saw my future husband. Gregg grew up down the road in Hooker-ton (yes, that's the name), a town of three hundred people, and he stood head and shoulders over his peers at six feet, six inches tall. His father was in the construction business and built houses. While it by no means made him a for-tune, it was enough to send Gregg to private school where he could focus on using his height and preternatural athlet-icism to dominate local sports.

Being a cheerleader, I didn't like him. He wasn't just tall, he was *good*—and good-looking, to add insult to injury. He played for our rival school, Parrott Academy, and our school didn't have that kind of talent, so there was no hope of ever beating his team. He was the king of that high school. Everyone knew what kind of car he drove. I remember seeing him cruising around town, looking for who-knows-what who-knows-where. As handsome as he was, I knew he was trouble.

But not me. I was going to college. My parents didn't have the money for it, but the church provided a scholarship to the University of Mount Olive in Mount Olive, North Carolina, pickle capital of the world.

Yes, you read that right. The world capital of pickles. Every year, they host a Mount Olive Pickle Classic, which is a bit like a briny homecoming. I'm very proud to say that I reigned as the 1975 Mount Olive Pickle Classic Queen. (To say it's been my crowning achievement might be a bit of an overstatement, but the pickles were delicious.) Much like my high school days, this ended up mattering significantly because, while I was making a name for myself as a Pickle Queen-slash-cheerleader, Gregg, who had gone to a different college to play basketball, was making his own way back to me. I was working at the Southern Belle Hotel Café when I heard a group of men talking about the famous Gregg Hill coming to Mount Olive to play for our team. Apparently, a cousin had talked him into transferring, and one day while I was hanging up pep posters in the hallway, I turned around, and there he was.

"I know you," he said.

That was the night I went where everyone from school went to have fun, Weil's Pizza Palace in Goldsboro. He walked straight up to me and asked me why I was drinking Pepsi. I told him I didn't drink alcohol.

"Wow," he said. "I've never met a girl like you."

Later that night, he told me he was going to marry me.

Sure, he was handsome. Sure, he was a bit of a wild man. But when Gregg and his friends would come to my dorm after partying all night, I'd griddle them all up sandwiches. We were both young and stupid. We were both growing up and discovering the dual sides of freedom. On the last day of school, Mama saw that Gregg had been drinking, and that might have been the only full-on spat she and I ever had. But you'd better believe she never saw him that way again. She wasn't particular about much, but even when she was, she was patient. One of the best things she and Daddy did was give Gregg and me time to become our own people.

I was in love with Gregg. Past the parties and the popularity, I saw something deep inside him that I genuinely couldn't be without. There was a plan for us, even back then. After a year of him telling me that we were going to be married, we finally made it happen on September 26, 1976. Mama went all-out on an elaborate, three-tiered wedding cake, and only years later did I learn that after one of the layers fell, she stayed up late the night before to fix it. She never mentioned anything to me. She never complained or acted the least bit tired. She'd given me all the love and support a daughter could ask for, and she sent me off seamlessly into my brand-new life.

Gregg and I hit the ground running after that. He started working with his father's construction company, expanding from barns and houses to (of all things) health-care facilities. His growing success allowed me to do what I'd always wanted—stay home and raise a family. Five kids later, I was living the dream in all its guts and glory. Gregg's business was booming, so all the diaper-changing, feeding, and toy-wrangling landed in my court. Our newlywed home quickly became a whirlwind of beautiful chaos as we crafted our household from the bottom up. I always wanted to open my own day-care center, and Mama assured me that I already had done so with my own wild bunch of kids.

And all the while, Mama was there. The deliveries, the babysitting, the birthdays . . . every major milestone involves some memory of her and her quiet strength. My kids all vividly recall her gorgeous cakes, making them their teachers' favorites, just as they'd done for me so many years before—train cakes, doll cakes, North Carolina cakes, cakes in the shape of famous landmarks . . . anything my kids needed, she somehow magically crafted. She never asked for thanks. She never made any demands of her own. If there was a baby who needed rocking or a school project that needed a little extra glitz, she was right on the job.

In her own humble, loving way, Mama became my most powerful supporter. She never told me how to raise my kids, never corrected me or even suggested that a fussy baby might be cold or hungry. One day, cranky and exhausted, I was hollering at the kids, when my son Gray turned around and told me, "Grandma Gray would never do that."

Wisdom from the mouth of babes, I know. But at the time, I wasn't having it.

"Why?" I shot back. "What makes you think she wouldn't do that?"

That child stood a little straighter, and with a stiff upper lip, said, "Because she knows the Lord."

Grandma Gray became a rock in their lives, an ever-present source of love and stability. Boy Scouts? Youth group? School pageant? She was right there participating however she could. My daughters Brittany and Lauren were obsessed with the song "So Long, Farewell" from *The Sound of Music*. Mama would sing it with them, over and over again, as they pretended to be the von Trapp girls traipsing up and down the last three steps to the family room. My youngest son, Drew, took an interest in gardening, so Mama helped him plant his own little gardens and pickle the vegetables he grew.

My mother was my kids' safe haven. When my daughter Lauren got mad, she would always threaten, "I'm going to call GrandMama and tell her to come get me!"

"Good!" my husband and I would reply. "Call her."

As frustrated parents, we were all for it.

Grade school angst aside, we were thankful for Mama being that safe, happy place for our kids. My parents made my children feel so important and loved—like they were the best kids on earth who could do no wrong.

Growing up with my mama and daddy practically right down the street was a dream come true. Of course, I took it for granted. I was raising my kids in the same community I'd grown up in. My family (with Mama in the lead, of course) have always been the kind of people to rush over to help. We were church people. Community people. My son Gregg played baby Jesus in the annual Christmas pageant, which Mama absolutely loved. Those first few years could have been straight out of a Hallmark movie.

Then came tennis, and Lord knows we had no idea how *that* one sport would change everything. My oldest son, Gregg, was born with fire under his feet. He was a high-strung and wild little boy, so we put him in every activity we could to help manage his energy levels. When he was about five, we found a little tennis clinic in Kinston, North Carolina. Gregg loved it—it had him running up and down the court for hours on end—so we decided to go forward with lessons. It wasn't long until the coaches started coming to me, delighted and bamboozled.

"Marsha," one of them finally told me, "that boy can hit the ball with the right hand and the left hand. I don't know what to do."

My husband and I didn't know what to do either. Tennis was a strange and foreign sport to us. We'd always seen it as a game for rich people. But as our fortunes started turning, we found ourselves in a whole new world. Gregg loved the game—and he was *good* at it. By the time he was eight, we were putting him on a plane to fly down to Hendersonville, North Carolina, for weekends of professional coaching. By the time he was nine, he had his sights fixed on the US Open. And by the time he hit the fifth grade, he wanted to live at the Bollettieri Tennis Academy in Bradenton, Florida. Mama and Daddy would often go stay with him, but even between me, my husband, and my parents rotating, it was hard to juggle time between the academy and North Carolina.

Our family had some big decisions to make. When your ten-year-old is on the fast track to becoming a professional athlete, life gets a bit more complicated. I wasn't entirely sure how a tennis career was supposed to fit into our hectic Hallmark life, but I knew I wasn't about to let my son move to Florida full-time to live on his own.

The solution ended up being a giant Southwind camper. While my husband continued to build his business, I packed my kids into that rolling behemoth and made the twelve-hour drive back and forth from Florida. And believe me when I say I had no idea what kind of mother I was until I was driving a twenty-four-foot vehicle down I-95 with five squalling children in the back.

Mama rode along with us on many of these adventures. She knew I was stressed, and she heard me hollering back at my kids to stop doing this or that or to get out of the bathroom more times than I'd care to admit. But she never scolded me for losing my temper. She never told me not to raise my voice or shamed me for being stressed or angry. She sat there quietly and let me mother my kids in my own way. I was a sopping puddle of nerves whenever we'd finally get to where we were going, but she would just mutter prayers to herself: "*Thank you, God. Thank you.*"

She was a marvel even back then. She didn't enforce a standard of discipline; she set the example. I see now just how countercultural she was to believe so strongly in giving people space and allowing them to take personal responsibility for the way they wanted to live their lives. Nowadays, it's common to hear advice about parenting to children's individual personalities and giving them room to be themselves, but back then, it was all about correction with the belt.

Mama was never that way. She gave my kids room to grow into themselves just like she gave me room to grow into motherhood. Again, I didn't see this or appreciate it at that time. But now, I couldn't be more thankful.

You never see the little miracles like that until you're looking at them in the rearview mirror. Every part of your life—every seemingly random piece of your story—ends up coming together in the most beautiful, unexpected ways. Both my parents played a massive role in helping me with my kids, and I didn't realize just how significant that would be until much later. At the time, I only saw what I needed and how they were helping me. There was no way I could have predicted how that would come full circle.

Take Gregg's tennis career, for instance. When our youngest, Drew, also fell for the sport, he wanted to train in Florida as well. Eventually, it became clear to us that we couldn't keep making the trek back and forth, so we decided to move the whole family. We packed up everything and left the only community we've ever known, and to say it was a culture shock would be a complete understatement. By this time, Gregg's tennis career moved him from Bradenton to Boca Raton. Here was a world where kids went to school with designer bags and sneakers worth more than most folks made in a week. Sure, our family was on the up and up as my husband's business expanded. But we weren't raised that way, and we took great care to ensure our kids weren't either. I was pretty proud when they came home from school disgusted and confused by the ostentatious shows of wealth and materialism.

But this was Boca Raton, and Boca Raton was tennis. I felt lonely and adrift, but I didn't realize just what a toll it took on my parents. We were used to having them down the street, meeting them every Wednesday at our favorite barbecue joint, Ken's Grill. They came down to visit us often, but things weren't the same.

Meanwhile, our son Gregg was enjoying a long and successful tennis career, but with it came inevitable injuries from exertion and overuse. When traditional treatments failed him, he sought alternative therapies and medicines, and this was far before essential oils and superfruit smoothies were common household products. For me, it was more than the treatment. It was about the mindset, the idea that just because the doctor tells you that you've hit a roadblock doesn't mean there's nothing else you can do. Gregg's experience with alternative sports medicine introduced me to the concept and expanded my horizons. I saw it working for him throughout his career. Why couldn't it work for the rest of my family elsewhere?

Throughout my childhood, my mama and daddy had always taken the stance that figures in authority were meant to be there. Whatever the doctor said was what you did because, well . . . they're the doctor. It wasn't that choosing alternative medicine was a form of rebellion or a blatant distrust of all modern medical practice. It was more of a mindset shift, an experience that planted one important and persistent question in the back of my mind: *Is there something else we can try?*

I'd always had a feeling something was wrong with Daddy, but we didn't find out he was a diabetic until he was in his forties. He would never go to the doctor for it, not until he collapsed on the road one day. His father and his sister both had histories with diabetes, and when a sore developed on his foot, we only connected the dots when the spot became gangrenous. I've always been squeamish around blood and death, but my daughter Brittany was born with a healer's heart, just like Mama. She wanted to help, so Mama taught her how to give Daddy his insulin shots, making her practice on an orange until she was ready to give them directly to her granddaddy.

I always say this was the beginning of my daughter's medical career. Years later, when Brittany graduated from physician assistant school, she chose to honor Mama in her white coat ceremony. Ironically enough, my mother letting my daughter do this small, seemingly insignificant thing might have been what set her on the path to being such a godsend throughout the pandemic.

But I'm getting ahead of myself.

Daddy's sore got worse, and the doctors offered a grim prognosis: they were going to have to amputate his entire foot. I remember getting that desperate call from North Carolina. Daddy was tough, and he wasn't scared of much. But he knew that if they took his foot, there would only be more amputations to follow if (some would say when) the surgery didn't heal right.

"Please," he begged me, "Marsha, don't let them take my foot off. The next thing to go is my leg."

So there I was, hundreds of miles away, panicking about what to do and how to take care of my daddy. It finally occurred to me to call my son Gregg and ask if he'd heard of any alternative treatment. As luck would have it, Gregg had been in contact with a practitioner using ozone treatments to help injured tennis players. I started bringing Daddy down to Florida to see this doctor, and he explained how a similar treatment could help save the gangrenous foot.

As much as I wanted to keep him under my watch, Daddy hated being away from home when he was sick. He wanted to be back in North Carolina at his own house in his own community. We found an alternative doctor in Jacksonville, North Carolina, willing to help with the treatment. Then we purchased a machine to make ozone water for his foot baths and found a way to use a peripherally inserted central catheter (commonly called a PICC line) to get him what he needed. Mama was his full-time caretaker, giving him multiple daily footbaths and ensuring he got through all of his treatments. She was just as wonderful of a nurse to him as she was to everyone else. Miraculously, the ozone treatment ended up completely healing his foot.

Between Gregg and Daddy, I was sold. I'd seen firsthand that dead-end roads aren't the *only* roads, that expanding your options and seeking alternative solutions are always worth fighting for. Gregg introduced me to yoga and acupuncture, and after my own horrific incident being put on the wrong medication, I sought Chinese herbal treatments from a local alternative physician in my community.

I had experienced multiple traumas over a short period of time, topped with a doctor misdiagnosing me, and I struggled for several hard months. I was trying so hard to take care of Mama and couldn't let her know the dark place I was in. That's when my son suggested I try acupuncture. I found Dr. Chen, and she was a blessing in my life. Mama also benefited from alternative medicine. When I moved her to Florida, she was on many medications and was having horrible headaches. I started taking her to Dr. Chen, who slowly started introducing herbs to her. Eventually, Mama was able to get off her medications completely, and her blood work was always perfect. I sent her to Dr. Chen weekly for acupuncture, and the results were life-changing. When Mama would have an EKG, the doctor would always wave it in the air and announce that she had the heart of a thirty-two-year-old. The dementia is what ultimately ended up slowing her down.

You would think that being raised in a religious home in rural North Carolina, Mama would have a thing or two to say about alternative therapy and Chinese medicine. But Mama didn't bat an eyelash. She took that doctor's herbs until the day she died, never once making a comment about differences in culture or religion. That could have had a lot to do with her natural trust of authority, but it also spoke a great deal to her trust in me. She was always open, always willing to try something new.

It's funny how God puts these little miracles in your life. It's hard to see them in the everyday hustle and bustle, but they're there. They might not be burning bushes or rains of frogs, but their quiet, humble workings leave me marveling just the same. Gregg getting into alternative treatments, Brittany discovering her love of care and healing by learning to give her granddaddy his insulin shots . . . there was no way to see how all these little pieces would eventually come together.

But it's truly the quiet miracles that are the most staggering, much like it's the quiet people who are the most influential. It's only natural not to appreciate the people we love when we have them, to be so caught up in the hustle and bustle of our own lives that we come to expect them as a constant rather than a timely blessing. We don't see the way the little things work together, the way the strongest of us are often the quietest and most gentle.

When I was in the midst of my own mothering misadventures, it was easy to feel inadequate or less-than when I compared myself to my mother. But now that she's gone, I can see all the things I've missed—the small, silent places she showed up to support me and let me come into my own. As natural as it is to grow up and away from our mothers, I also think it's natural to marvel at them, especially when we look back and realize all the little miracles we missed. In their presence, we feel their love, but only in their absence do we feel how extraordinary they truly were.

7

Life, Death, and Taxes

There are few things we can count on in this world. As the old adage goes, "life, death, and taxes" seem to be the only sure things. Nothing rubbed that in more than the COVID pandemic. All of a sudden, the jobs we'd always worked, the friends we'd always seen, the routines we were so used to, and even the items we'd always assumed would stock the shelves of our grocery stores were gone.

It was a jarring time of death and confusion, but even for those who didn't know any COVID victims personally, there was still trauma on a scale I don't think we fully understand. I'm talking community trauma. *Global trauma.* A society interrupted. When the world opened back up, we had a generation of kids who'd never stepped foot into an actual classroom, bedraggled parents who'd been working overtime as homeschool teachers, and essential workers whose very normal, very safe jobs suddenly became a question of life and death.

You didn't have to lose anyone during the pandemic to have felt this. That's what makes this time so strange and terrifying. Nowadays, we joke about toilet paper and have masks readily available pretty much everywhere we go, but I don't think we have a clue just how deep this societal trauma goes.

And trust me, I get it. No one wants to talk about the bad times. No one wants to dwell on the pain and confusion after being homebound and scared for so long. Our human brains do this amazing thing where we file the uncomfortable memories way in the back, forbidden and, hopefully, eventually, forgotten. You don't remember the pain of giving birth. Your brain can't handle that. It filters out the agony and the fear and keeps the memories you want, the joy and delight of new life. Having had five kids myself, let me tell you that no one is more grateful for this handy-dandy brain trick than I am. If ignorance is bliss, then *forgetting altogether* has to be paradise.

But there's a danger to this. Obliviousness—collective forgetting, stuffing down trauma in hopes of banishing it forever—not only sets us up for deep-seated issues. It also runs the risk of giving us exactly what we want: ignorance.

Living through COVID was uncomfortable at best but earthshattering for most. That level of collective trauma can only be ignored at our own risk. There are still wounds to be healed and lessons to be learned. We worry for the children behind in their schoolwork, the essential workers strung out and overworked, the homeless and those living in poverty, those with mental health issues, and countless other vulnerable and/or marginalized people. By nature, I am always overly concerned about children. My grandchildren are fortunate in that they were in schools that opened quickly, and they have had access to tutors to catch up. We all know many kids are far less fortunate and are behind and may not be able to catch up. I suspect we will see the effects of COVID and its aftermath for many generations to come. We could choose not to think about these things. We could take the attitude that what happened, happened, those who survived were meant to, and since life has gone back to "normal," we don't have to sort through the rubble or relive the experience.

Talking about what happened to our most vulnerable populations isn't something you can do in a vacuum. It brings up *all* the trauma, and that's a heavy burden to lift. But by not talking about these issues, we're ensuring that we keep the vulnerable, vulnerable. We won't learn from our mistakes. We won't do anything differently in the future. As much as we think that wealth, status, and power can shield us from things like poverty and homelessness, there is one thing none of us can avoid, as inevitable as life, death, and taxes: getting older. The elderly are some of the most vulnerable people in our society, and the ironic thing is, most of us are destined to become a part of the demographic.

I get where the discrimination comes from. When we think of retirement communities, we see images of bridge tables and golf carts, grumpy old men and shriveled little women driving unbearably below the speed limit on a two-lane road. Our modern American society is a society that doesn't value the elderly, and it's important to think about why that is. Back in the day, the elders of the town or village would have been the center of knowledge, the accumulation of experience, culture, and wisdom collected through the ages. Ancient cultures, notably the Greeks, revered the elderly for their collective knowledge. Senior citizens were valued; they had a concrete role in society.

Our attitude has shifted over these last thousand or so years. Disease and declining health have been linked to old age, so we associate the aged with the decrepit, something used up and disposable with no value or purpose. And this isn't to say this is the fault of any one generation or blame a certain age group. This isn't the fault of "the youth," but it's not the fault of the aged either. This is a *collective* attitude, a societal view that we've washed, rinsed, and recycled for centuries. We can sit here and complain about Social Security or the unprecedented rise in the senior population, but as we ourselves age, what are we doing to bring value to our communities? How are we meeting the next generation to pass on our wisdom and experience?

From what I've seen, generational selfishness goes both ways. The younger generation is quick to discard the elderly as useless and burdensome, but as that same generation matures, they're not asking how, in their own old age, they can be different.

And so the cycle continues, round and round. Plodding across time as steady as life, death, and taxes.

When there's an issue of child abuse, you'll see a whole community rise up in an uproar. And rightfully so. Children have potential. They have their whole lives to contribute to society and make an impact on our world. The elderly, on the other hand, are much easier to dismiss. Even though many of them are as helpless as children, they don't have the same future. We take the attitude that they're just going to die anyway. What's the point of fighting for them?

I never realized this until I experienced it firsthand. Hospitals are life and death machines. If women are expected to give birth on a schedule, it's no wonder that the elderly are supposed to die on schedule too.

I was twenty when I had my first child. Nobody told me about what I was facing. My mama was very modest; she never went into detail with me. I had no idea what to expect, what it would feel like or how to advocate for my health. These days, birthing classes and talking about birth are much more normalized. Doulas, Lamaze, birthing plans . . . there are so many more resources for new mothers than I had when I first gave birth.

Unsurprisingly, you don't see as many advocacy resources when it comes to caring for the elderly. Working through both my mama and daddy's health issues constantly felt like a frantic game of catch-up. The treatments they received were mostly symptom-based and didn't often push to the root of the problem. This issue grew from annoying to downright ridiculous. The physicians were ready to ship Mama off to a rehab facility. What she needed instead was a certain back procedure.

While caring for my parents, I was advised again and again to be there with them throughout the process, even if that meant simply getting on the phone and talking about what the doctor had told them at their appointment. My parents didn't know how to advocate for themselves. They'd been raised to trust the preacher and the doctor without question. Heck, *I* didn't know how to advocate for them. It took hours of frenzied research, sleepless nights of debating cures and options to find the best way forward.

Many doctors don't have (or take) that kind of time. The culture of Western consumerism has made our medical system the monster it is today. Treat the symptom, collect the money, and move on to the next patient. Taking time to actually treat an elderly person—to treat the disease and not just the symptoms, to look at healing rather than just managing pain even when the patient might not have long to live—clogs the machine. It is often not the fault of the individual medical providers; they are overworked and exhausted and are doing the best they can while being part of a very flawed system.

Mama was always very brave. Death didn't scare her. Neither did pain. She was a grown woman with indomitable faith. But as she aged, that changed. I watched her go from a strong, confident woman to a frightened child. She couldn't remember where she was. She couldn't remember what had happened the day before. So to wake up in a hospital, to be there alone and confused, was traumatizing. She was in a strange place with strange people touching her, telling her about medicines and procedures she couldn't possibly keep track of. In a lot of ways, the psychological trauma made more of an impact than the physical trauma.

That's why I knew I had to stay with Mama if and when she ended up in the hospital. I had to be there for her, to hold her hand, sing to her, or simply keep touching her shoulder so she knew someone was there for her. Part of her healing was feeling safe and comfortable.

When COVID hit, staying with Mama was no longer an option. When the lockdowns started, the health-care facilities and hospitals did what they had to. Residents were quarantined or relocated to special wings. Extreme measures were put into place. But like children, a lot of these seniors had no idea what was going on. They didn't understand why these measures were in place. They were scared, confused, and upset every time they woke up. We all remember what it was like to have our world flipped upside-down. Imagine experiencing that *every single morning.*

It was a fearful time for everyone, but that fear was different for the elderly.

With as vulnerable as the patients were, many staff ended up not coming into work or quitting their jobs entirely. There was such a lack of personal protective equipment, my husband ended up hiring workers to make more masks. With families forced to keep their children at home, many having to care for their kids on top of working full-time jobs, how was anyone expected to do the same for elderly family members? Seniors who needed constant supervision? Diaper changes? Routine medicine and special diets?

The lockdowns were brutal for everyone, but especially for the elderly in health-care facilities. Physically quarantining mitigated the risk. But the psychological neglect, the trauma to the mind and soul, had to have been just as grueling. There was no way to measure the impact of the fright, panic, and depression.

I try to imagine doing that to my child. If, for instance, instead of sending children home, the government had demanded that we quarantine kids in their classrooms and forbidden parents from visiting them. I can't imagine not being able to hold my babies in a situation like that, a situation where they would be scared, confused, lonely, and hurting. I can't imagine it because I don't *want* to imagine it.

Maybe this is why it's so easy to purge our collective memories, to brush off, forget, or even ignore the reality for seniors in hospitals and health-care facilities during the pandemic. All throughout COVID, I took care of my mother because I could. I had the time, money, and resources. Unlike so many, I could advocate for her dignity and go out of my way to secure her small comforts.

Losing my mother the way I did was one of the most traumatic events of my life. Years later, I still dream about her lying there, rasping on her pillow, so weak she can't even swallow or hold her head up. But for many elderly victims, there was no one weeping for them as they struggled to breathe. No one came to comfort them when they broke down in tears, frightened and alone, not knowing where they were.

I fought for my mother until the very end. But what about the millions of seniors who didn't have a Marsha? Who didn't have anyone advocating for them? Because they're elderly, does that mean they deserve to be discarded like that? And if so, what does that mean for our future?

These are the questions that haunt me, the questions that keep me up late into the night, thinking about Mama. They're not fun questions. Take it from me, they don't make for a peaceful night of sleep. But if we don't ask these questions—if we ignore them because they're ugly, tragic, and uncomfortable—we're setting the stage for the very same future.

We all want a long, healthy life. We pray for it, exercise our bodies, eat right, and take our vitamins hoping that good health will afford us more time with the people we love. But just like life, death, and taxes, that long life also comes with complications. Living long means *aging*, plain and simple, and as much as we'd like to have one without the other, COVID showed us the side of longevity that most of us don't like to acknowledge. Decrepitude. Breakdown. A reversion back to childlike helplessness.

As the world settles into the light of its new normal, no one wants to venture back into the darkness. But we have to, not just for the ones we've loved and lost.

We have to go there for ourselves.

8

My Great

ife is made up of polarities. Day and night, old and young, summer and winter . . . it's so easy to look around and draw the conclusion that everything is made up of opposing forces. You can't turn on the TV these days without hearing about one extreme battling the other.

In a lot of ways, it's simpler to look at life as black and white or take on an "us versus them" mentality. Of course, that's not to say there aren't fights worth fighting, but that's the thing about righteous anger and sweeping change. They come about because of *imbalance*, a shameless slant to one side, which creates a situation of unfairness or inequity that requires correction and change. Strong emotions are what rally us when crooked members of society prey on the weak. These emotions serve us when there are wrongs that need righted.

I'm not saying that being angry or taking up a grievance is a bad thing. However, I'm also not saying it's an inherently good one either. Like any other effort in this world, adjustment requires hard work and effort. But it's completely possible to be so consumed by that effort that you lose sight of why you were adjusting in the first place.

Life is a push and pull of just about everything—anger and peace, work and rest, and even birth and death. We love to think in these extremes because they're solid and easy to define. It's everything in the middle that gets muddy. Between black and white, happiness and despair, the old and the young, lies an endless spectrum of chance, opportunity, and experience. We all know we're born and will inevitably die. It's easy enough to grasp that the young will grow up and eventually become old. But the time in between isn't so easy. It's no simple task to determine which shade of gray is the official median between "more-black-than-white" and "more-white-than-black." At what point does growing up turn into growing old? And when does aging turn from an upward slope to a downward one?

As living beings, we're constantly in motion. We're growing, changing, and adjusting to new seasons in life. We can't truly stop changing because the world around us never stops changing. When it gets cold outside, you put on a sweater. When the sweltering summer heat starts up again, you take the sweater off. Maybe we feel settled or content at a particular time or in a particular area of our lives, but just because we feel like we've reached a balance doesn't mean the change isn't happening.

For me, it's these long, creeping changes that are the most beautiful and gruesome. Aging brings incredible joys like wisdom and watching your children's children grow. It also comes with a host of other not-so-pleasant experiences, particularly the aches and pains that seem to crop up on the daily. I'm so thankful I got to be with my mother during the last years of her life, but being with her also made it hard to see how much she was changing and how those changes affected her. If you see a houseplant in your kitchen every morning, it seems to grow much slower than a plant you see every few months. And as Grandma Adaline became Great-Grandma Adaline (and eventually "Great Nine," the name the great-grandkids called her), those little, slinking changes went from adorable wrinkles and stories on repeat to real, painful loss. I wish I knew when the switch flipped. I wish I could tell you exactly when the cycle of life turns from growth to decline.

But that's the problem with thinking in extremes. Life isn't ever *just* growth or *just* decay. Aging is far too complex to boil down to polarities. Every stage of life has its own joy just as every stage of life has its own challenges. It's not about finding a "sweet spot" and staying there; it's about finding the sweet spot wherever you are. If life is a game of push and pull, we've got to find a way to be happy in-between.

Mama aged gracefully—no one would argue that—and I know she was full of joy in every stage of her life. However, that doesn't mean that getting older wasn't without its challenges, even for a saint like her. My mother had selflessly served others her whole life. She was always the one providing, always working, cooking, sewing, and attending to everyone else's needs. Suddenly (and I say "suddenly" because it *is* sudden, like the plant you haven't seen in months), she found herself in a place where she *couldn't* be the person she'd been her whole life. Like everything else, her physical and mental capacities were changing.

But no one flipped a switch. She never woke up on a random morning and said, "Well, I'm elderly now. I guess it's time to slow down." Of course, we feel those aches and pains as the years go by. Maybe we even choose a set age to retire. But even that doesn't prepare us mentally for the challenges of getting old.

Someday, most of us will wake up in a body we aren't familiar with, a body that feels foreign and maybe even restrictive. Someday, most of us will wake up in a world we don't recognize, a culture marching along to a progressive pace that we're just too tired to match. And someday, the number of people who knew us as we knew ourselves— saw the world as we saw it and lived in the society we remember—is going to start dwindling.

We can take vitamins, get antiaging injections, and play puzzle games as much as we want. But will any anti-aging effort ever prepare us for *that*?

Life is a weird push and pull no matter what age you are. Every new parent jokes about their infant changing their diapers someday, but we don't tend to dwell on that reality any more than we have to. If our parents give us so much of their lives, what's our obligation to give back to them as children? As a *society*? And what does the transition from the caretaker to the one cared for even look like?

Like I said, it would be so much easier if there were a magical switch that flipped whenever you reached a new stage of life. But the truth is, we don't know what it means to be an elderly person any more than we know what it means to be a child. Even with wonderful parents like mine, these are tough waters to navigate. Mama and Daddy were always kind and gracious, but getting to the point where my husband and I had to care for them was a difficult adjustment. They were so used to caring for others, so used to making things work and pulling themselves up by their bootstraps—not to mention how horrible they were at taking care of themselves. But they didn't come from a generation that valued self-care. When they reached the age when taking care of themselves became critical, is it any wonder they were so bad at it?

My parents were trusting, selfless people who believed in the good of humanity. And while these are certainly noble traits, I couldn't sleep easy after leaving them behind to move to Florida for my son's tennis career. Of course, Mama and Daddy were extremely competent people. By no means did I doubt their intelligence. It was their sense of humility that worried me, their inherent hesitation to do anything that might be perceived as "being a burden." And while nothing bristles my feathers more than entitlement, the opposite end of the spectrum can be just as troubling.

One year after we'd left for Florida, Mama and Daddy got dangerously ill with the flu. I had no idea until I pressed her on the subject. I could tell over the phone that something was wrong. Even when my dad was on his deathbed, Mama would only ever report that he was "doing OK" whenever I called. That may be the only white lie that Adaline Gray ever told. She didn't want me rushing out there. She didn't want to burden me, even when it came down to dire need.

This is what made taking care of her and Daddy so frustrating. On one hand, my family in Florida needed me as a wife and mother, and I know my parents didn't want to bother me to care for them as well. But them not wanting to be a bother bothered me more because I was never sure if I would call to find them perfectly fine or half-dead and quietly starving so as not to inconvenience anyone.

I wanted to care for my parents. It meant the world to give back to them, especially when they'd given so much to me. But leaving them behind to move to Boca Raton had me caught between generations in a strange way I wasn't prepared to deal with.

We all want what's best for our kids. We want them to be successful and craft lives better than the ones we lived. But no one teaches you how to *live* in that situation when it becomes reality.

Over the years, my husband's business thrived, so much so that we had the means to care for my parents financially. Gregg also ended up growing closer to Mama and Daddy than he ever had been to his own parents. On Christmas Day 1993, he gifted Daddy the dream car he'd always wanted, but had never been able to afford—a Lincoln

Continental. Daddy was never one to show much emotion, but he cried that day. He loved and cherished that car, and he was loath to let Mama drive it. She was good at many things, but one of her infamous peccadilloes was that she drove with both her feet.

The car was a dream, but not having their grandkids down the street was what really took a toll on them. That was apparent with every phone call and visit. But my parents never complained or criticized Gregg and me for our decision to move to Florida. Like always, Mama and Daddy were quiet supporters, and even when Daddy's health began to decline, she never asked for help, even when he ended up in the hospital. When things started getting really bad, my Uncle Amos proposed scheduled watches so everyone could cycle in and out of Daddy's hospital room and get some sleep. But Mama refused.

"I'm going to be here the whole time," she said. "And there's no way I'm putting my children on any sort of schedule."

She stayed by Daddy's side, even when the nurses were telling her to leave. She was there when he died on April 22, 1999. They'd been married fifty-one years.

In the throes of mourning my father, it hit me hard that I now had new worries about my mother. Sure, she and Daddy would drag themselves to death's door without even considering inconveniencing anyone, but at least they had each other. Now, my elderly mother would be completely by herself. And at the age of seventy-four, that wasn't something I was comfortable with.

Shortly after Daddy died, I made the decision to move Mama down with the family to Florida. She never questioned me; she never rebelled or harbored any bitterness about being uprooted from the only home she'd ever known. At first, it was a back-and-forth situation, but it wasn't long before we had to arrange for her to stay with us full-time.

Mama's four sisters—Helen, Jean, Kay, and Alice— had no qualms with voicing their opinions about the matter, and they were none too pleased with the separation. "South Florida isn't a collards and grits kind of place," one of them told me.

I know they meant well. I adore them. They truly wanted what was best for Mama, and so did I. But at the time, I was sensitive to criticism because *I* didn't feel completely confident in my own decision. The last thing I wanted was to uproot Mama from her beloved home and community, but in my heart of hearts, I knew I had to take care of her no matter where we lived.

The decision was a heavy one, and there was no winning. I knew no one would be happy with any choice I made, so I did what I thought was best for Mama—which, at the end of the day, is what I truly believe was the right thing to do. I tried my best to make her as comfortable as possible, going out of my way to cook her favorite foods and finding pockets of the culture she'd left behind—restaurants, churches, anything that reminded her of North Carolina.

I'm sure the sisters weren't happy about that, and I do feel bad for them. But they all had extensive families of their own, and Mama was living by herself. But Mama never made a big deal about the move or leaving her sisters. She would often pick up the phone to check in with them, smiling gently as she repeated one of her all-time favorite phrases: "Thank God for Alexander Graham Bell."

By this time, our family of five was growing, and my life was filling up with grandchildren of my own. Mama had always been close with my kids (she always called my eldest "her firstborn"), and she delighted in seeing her great-grandbabies. One of her favorite things to do was sit at the piano with my youngest son, Drew, and sing hymns while he played. Some of my most cherished memories are the four generations gathered around that piano, singing together in harmony. That's not something you see every day.

"I'll see you tomorrow," she'd always say. "Lord willing and the creek don't rise."

Of course, the great-grandkids adored her. Adaline was a bit hard for them to pronounce, so based on the tradition one of Mama's younger nephews started years prior, the great-grandkids started calling her Great Nine. The nickname stuck. A lot of kids don't grow up knowing their great-grandparents, so my grandbabies having such a strong relationship with *my* mother was truly something special.

But even surrounded by family, Mama had trouble adjusting to her new life. She'd spent over seventy years in North Carolina. Florida wasn't her life; it wasn't her world. She'd come from a community she'd grown up with, where everyone knew all about her and her strong faith. I found a church outreach called Bibletown in Boca Raton, a Christian-based program that hosted faith-based events on the daily. I always felt a twinge of guilt dropping her off—like I was dumping her in an adult daycare—but she seemed happy. Her mental faculties were still pretty good at that point, so she could truly enjoy the people there and connect with them on a spiritual level.

Another woman who went to Bibletown, Miriam, became Mama's best friend. Miriam was a bit older than Mama, but they bonded over their faith and soon became inseparable. Miriam was a lot like Mama, but she'd never had children, and Mama worried about her not having anyone to take care of her. So naturally, Mama stepped right into the role of caretaker, companion, and best friend. The two did everything together. Certainly, this was a blessing for Miriam, but I think it was just as good for Mama. Her whole life, she'd been a caretaker. She'd always had a sibling, a husband, a baby, or a needy person in her community to serve. Miriam filled that void for her—at least for a little while. Taking care of her gave Mama purpose and reinforced her identity.

When they finally had to put Miriam in a facility, I remember Mama being so upset. Maybe it was because she knew this was an inevitable part of aging. Or maybe it hurt her so deeply because she wasn't able to care for someone so dear to her.

But Mama made the best of every situation. Her faith in God's divine plan and determination to find goodness, no matter how deep it was buried, had become something of a local family legend. But becoming a retiree, then a widow, and *then* moving away from her lifelong home was a triple blow. In 2000, we rented her a little apartment in a building with other seniors. There were nice people in the block, but just as many nasty ones. When Mama would dress up for church, whoever lived below her would complain about hearing her heels clicking on the tile floor. Mama was so scared of upsetting or offending anyone, she became terrified to get dressed.

Criticisms like that never angered her. They hurt her. Again, she never complained or spoke up to defend herself. As a true Southern, Free Will Baptist girl (when it comes to the South, Florida doesn't count), she just wasn't raised that way.

Some parts of Florida living took getting adjusted to, but there were just as many others she truly loved. One thing we both enjoyed together was my burgeoning amateur tennis career. I'd spent most of my time as a mother in the tennis world, but it wasn't until my early fifties that I actually had time to learn to play. You would think that years of watching my son would have rubbed some raw natural talent off on me, but unfortunately, that wasn't the case. I had to start at the bottom and work my way up.

Mama *loved* watching me play, and she came to every match. And as much as she loved to watch, I loved having her there. Our weekly games became the highlight of my week. The other women on my team fell head-over-heels in love with her, so much so that they started calling her Mama too. We bought her a uniform so she could match ours, and she would come to the matches wearing it. She became our rallying point—something of a mascot.

My team was pretty good, but we still lost a match now and then. Whenever we were losing, she would sit there in the stands with her eyes closed, praying for us to win. I have no idea if she could tell if we were winning or not. I'm not even sure she fully understood the rules.

"Mama," I'd tell her. "Maybe God doesn't want us to win today. Maybe it's his will for the other team to win."

But she would just sit there, eyes shut tight, and smile. "I'm still prayin'."

Having that team—building a community—was good for her, especially as the early stages of dementia began to set in.

Even before COVID, it was hard to watch. I could bring her to events, do everything I could to make her included, and surround her with family, but none of that could ease her loneliness or make the adjustments any easier. It wasn't just the change in location. It was also the change of roles, shaking her identity down to its very core. Her whole life, she'd had someone else to take care of, and when it came time to take care of herself, she struggled with the transition.

Maybe it was the way she was raised. Maybe it came down to religion or tradition. But looking back—looking at the dueling sides of selflessness and self-care—I see the sticky trap of extremes. In Mama's world, there wasn't a "me society" the way there is in my generation. Nowadays, people are better about setting boundaries and caring for themselves both physically and mentally. That's not a bad thing. From what I've seen, every generation, consciously or otherwise, is working to strike a balance for themselves.

I've always struggled with being able to live up to Mama's kindness and charity, but ironically, I'm just as bad at taking care of myself as she was. After a long list of life-altering traumas, it's no wonder that I finally shattered. For months, I was too scared to even leave my house. That's when I finally turned to taking care of myself and healing, not because I particularly wanted to, but because I *had* to.

Of course, I've heard all the adages about "putting your oxygen mask on before your neighbor's." Of course, I can *intellectually grasp* that you have to be healthy and capable in order to care of someone else. But when we're in the thick of life, driving exhausted with five kids down the highway at sixty-five-miles-an-hour in a giant camper, what you know you should be doing and what needs to be done in the moment are two different things.

If taking care of ourselves were convenient, we'd all be doing it. If living a healthy, balanced life were easy, we'd see a lot more healthy, balanced people.

Mama needed to focus on herself more. That was easy to see. But when I look out at today's rising generation of influencers and reality TV stars, it's just as apparent that they need to focus more on others.

Mama had never practiced self-care. When she aged into a season where she *had* to start caring for herself and letting others take care of her, she didn't know how to reconcile her new reality with the life she'd been living for the last seventy years. These days, we talk about self-care as a basic human right—and it should be. But how do we communicate that to a generation that didn't grow up with those values?

Life is a game of push and pull. We're always trying to do things a little better, always trying to find balance in our lives and in our communities. But how we view our own personal value and the value of self-care isn't black and white. It changes with time, evolves over seasons, and may even be influenced by where we live or how much money we have in the bank. We can absolutely say that self-care is a real and pressing necessity, but it would also be naïve to say that it's easy or even accessible.

I wish I could have helped my mother navigate the transition. I wish I could have gotten into her brain to know what she needed and what I could have done to make things easier on her. Life isn't about flipping switches; it's about doing our best with what we have whenever we happen to have it.

Maybe there's no hard-set date or scientific manual to tell us when the joys and struggles of aging are going to set in, but at the very least, we can open up a conversation with our aging loved ones. We can talk to them about taking care of themselves before it becomes critical, talk to them about loneliness, loss, and transition in a loving, supported, and safe place. If we're going to find a balance (dare I say, a *graceful* approach to getting old), we're going to need input from both sides. Not just for them, but for ourselves—our children and *their* children's children.

The fact is, we're all going to get old. The other fact is, none of us is truly prepared for the experience. And while we can't have perfect contingencies or protect ourselves completely from the pain of adjustment, we can strive to find joy in the balance.

9

A Family Affair

I t's impossible to talk about how our culture treats the elderly without discussing the modern family. The role and responsibilities of the family unit is always the elephant in the room when it comes to this topic, the *seemingly* simple solution to the problem. After all, haven't individual family units been traditionally responsible for caring for elderly members?

If you've seen the parts of American history I've seen, you'll remember a time when it was common for elderly parents to stay with their children as they aged. Thinking back to old black and white sitcoms, grandparents tended to be important family characters. A strong but silent tenant of the white-picket-fence American Dream was the centralization of the family unit. It seemed like—to me, anyway—that's just the way things were. Parents cared for their children, and children eventually turned around and returned the favor.

Of course, this is looking at the past through rose-colored glasses. Like everything discussed in this book, the family's role in taking care of the elderly isn't a simple issue. When you start talking through socioeconomics, regional and traditional cultures, medical complications, and family relationships (not to mention personal circumstances), each person being responsible and taking care of their respective parents isn't a clean solution. Even when I was a child, the burden of caring for the sick and aging was a sticky issue—an issue my mother, more often than not, dove right in to solve as best as she could. But Mama couldn't take care of everyone, even in her small, tight-knit community. It's never been reasonable to expect a one-to-one, quid-pro-quo arrangement like that. Life is too complicated, too unexpected.

So what can we expect?

That's also a thorny question, especially as the population lives longer and our world becomes more global. Nowadays, my kids live all over the place, and none of them have returned to where Gregg and I grew up. Besides being scattered to the winds, they also have their own children—their own lives—that keep them busy at all hours of the day. When I think about my own aging and how I want to be cared for when I can't care for myself, I understand where my mother was coming from. You don't want to be a burden. You don't want your kids to stop living their own lives to take care of you. But then . . . who's supposed to take care of you? What if your health declines so much they *can't* take care of you?

Everybody wants to go to heaven, but nobody wants to die. Nobody wants to be an inconvenience.

I'd always promised Mama that if she ever needed full-time care, she could still remain in her own home environment. There's a psychological aspect to that, losing your independence and coming to terms with your own mortality, but I'm sure it also had to do with the way she grew up. Back in her childhood, it was more common for families to take care of their own. She didn't want to inconvenience anyone, but after she retired and Daddy died, family was all she had left of who she'd been and the world she'd grown up in.

This was a big part of why we decided to put her up in her own apartment and hire help to come to her. Of course, we had the money and resources to do so; not all families have that luxury. But I wanted her to be right down the street so she could interact with her grandchildren and great-grandchildren as much as she could. She loved being Great Nine to them. She loved going to their activities and helping them work on school projects. My oldest grandson, Hill, absolutely adored her. He was especially loving and attentive, even if that meant simply holding her hand or sitting beside her so she knew someone was there. The whole family would come over to celebrate the holidays with her and belt out her favorite hymns around the piano. We even threw her a giant surprise bash on her seventy-fifth birthday, complete with an outpouring of loving letters and well-wishes from people she'd touched throughout her life. No matter how old she got, I went out of my way to make her a central part of our world. My husband even ended up naming his boat *Sweet Adaline* in her honor.

In her last years, I wanted Mama living with our family. I wanted her to know that no matter how much the world changed, she would always be loved.

The global pandemic had a funny way of disregarding our plans—even plans we'd been making for years. But ironically enough, through all the fear and chaos of COVID, family ended up being the only thing we could rely on. Of course, I include Regina, Mama's courageous caretaker, and Javier, her nurse, in those numbers. After going through everything with us, they've become just as close as blood relatives. When it came down to the wire, it was family who showed up to help—family who put themselves second and even risked their physical safety to be there for Mama. You may make plans to live forever or micromanage every minute detail of your life, but when you finally reach the end of your journey, family (blood-related or not) is all you have.

When we were dealing with trying to get Mama oxygen and knew she was going downhill, my boys dropped everything to travel to her apartment and see her. Even though we didn't have positive confirmation for COVID, Gray and Drew wasted no time getting masked up and into proper PPE so they could be by their grandmother's side. By that point, Mama was pretty far gone. I was talking to her and singing to her, but she didn't seem to register my voice. It often felt like she didn't even recognize me.

She wasn't showing any emotion. Most days, she could only gasp. But when those two boys walked in the room, I saw a spark as she raised her eyes to see who had come to visit.

"Mama," I said gently. "Graybie and Drewbie are here."

It was like watching a switch flip. She immediately recognized them and tried to sit up. They had to rush over to her and ease her back down. She was so weak, so confused, and in so much pain. But she knew who they were. That flash of recognition, of love and understanding, said more than words ever could. Drew ended up having to quarantine in his office for two weeks after that visit, but he didn't hesitate for a second.

Later, my third son, Gregg, came by with his children. They'd made bright, colored posters sharing how much they loved Mama and how they were praying for her to get well. My daughter Lauren was all set to fly to Florida to say "goodbye," but at the last second her youngest daughter spiked a high fever. We all know what fever meant at that time—the possibility of COVID. At that time, we didn't know Mama had COVID, so Lauren stayed behind in an attempt to protect Mama from getting COVID. In retrospect, this was a God thing. Lauren is like me when it comes to sickness, medicines, needles, blood, and death. She and I both can't handle it. Mama knew that. All of this is to say that when the doctor wasn't answering his phone and couldn't even make hospice arrangements, my kids showed up.

When we finally learned Mama was COVID positive, we also learned that hospice protocols were different due to the pandemic.

Therefore, Mama never even had a proper hospice evaluation or assessment of her needs. Morphine was dropped off at the apartment door.

In other words, morphine. Morphine to help her die. As Mama's chest rattled and her breathing got even shallower, there was no escaping the choice we had to make. Either we let the suffering go on, or we make the decision to let go.

That day, I asked my mother the same question I'd been asking her for years. "Mama, are you ready to meet Jesus?"

She must have heard me. Her eyelids fluttered. She couldn't make a sound, but she didn't have to. I'd posed the same question to her so many times before. She was ready to go. The pain was too much.

My daughter Brittany ended up getting on a plane and flying out to help. She had young children at home and was still breastfeeding one of them, but she knew Mama needed her. She knew *I* needed her. I was sick, exasperated, and exhausted. I was just *so tired* of fighting for my baby.

But if there's anyone I want on my side during an impossible situation, it's Brittany. She came out to be with Mama during those last days, assisting Javier and Regina as they monitored her vitals and administrated the medication she needed to pass peacefully. When Brittany was at Mama's bedside, I kept flashing back to when she was a little girl learning how to give her granddaddy his insulin shots.

Even as a little girl, Brittany had always wanted to help care for people, just like her grandma. And there she was, so many years later, using that same passion and skill to help Mama. It was a strange thing to watch. Sad, but also heartwarming. After Mama died, Brittany would have to quarantine far away from her children for another two weeks. It was a sacrifice to be away from those little ones who absolutely adored her, but she didn't bat an eyelash when I called her for help.

At the very end, family was all we had.

It's impossible to say what the family's role should be when it comes to caring for the elderly. Everyone's situation is different, and when it comes to complications regarding resources, medical care, or even time and space to accommodate someone else's needs, there's no easy answer. But family *does* mean something. In our case, it meant everything. Of course, our situation was extreme and unprecedented, as were most during the pandemic. But that doesn't make my family's support any less important or miraculous.

Mama grew up in a time where families depended on one another. They had to. Communities contained people who lived close to and took care of one another for better or worse. It's amazing that Mama lived to see a different world, a world where you could connect over thousands of miles with the click of a button and wish every out-of-state grandchild goodnight without having to leave the living room couch. I think anyone, Mama especially, would say that's a beautiful thing.

Change, however, always comes with complications, and sometimes the most powerful consequences are the ones we don't consider. In our insta-connected, two-day delivery world, who takes care of the people who once took care of us? Who has the time or the resources to do so, and if it isn't the family, what does that mean for future generations?

There's no easy answer to these questions. COVID has shown us that even with all our technology and connections, there are circumstances we just can't predict. When doctors, hospitals, and even trusted friends failed us, our family stepped up for Mama. I'll never forget seeing my grandchildren singing to her outside her apartment window or watching my daughter draw up syringes the way she used to for my own father.

There are a few things I know to be sure in this life, and family is one of them. When you have family, whether that's blood-related kin or kin in spirit, you have a constant you can always depend on.

10

My Charge

When we think about getting old, we tend to be reductive. Most of us are OK with the overall image of aging—the graying hair, wrinkles, knee braces, and liver spots—but only if it applies to someone else. When we're young, aging seems distant, something we can happily ignore or dismiss as cosmetic. Our society has built a billion-dollar industry devoted to *anti*aging creams, fillers, surgeries, and even hormones to stave off the inevitable. Sure, old people are "cute," but we don't like to think about what's going on under the surface—or dwell on the idea that, someday, we're going to be in their same position.

Like all things in life, your relationship with your parents changes as they age, even more so when they transition into old age. You get so wrapped up in your own family and daily activities, it seems to happen in the blink of an eye. Of course, I knew my mama was aging. But I didn't see her as an *elderly person*—not until the physical changes began morphing into something much more serious.

It's easy to dismiss those deeper, unpleasant realities. It's easy to brush away your parent's forgetfulness or laugh it off when they begin to tell the same meandering story time and time again. Those subtler changes—the fact that it's not just their physical health, but also their mental faculties—are a whole different beast. Changes in your body are daunting enough to deal with, but what happens when your own mind starts betraying you?

That is a truly terrifying thought, not just for the elderly, but also for their caretakers. All the time you're running around trying to take care of your own family, you realize you're running against a ticking clock. Sooner or later, you're going to have to figure out how to take care of your aging loved one on top of everything else in your life. I know that sounds selfish, but it's the reality of our society. If your parents live long enough, they're eventually going to need care and assistance, accommodations that require time, money, and, more often than not, extreme amounts of energy. While kids grow up and become more independent, the level of care and responsibility required to take care of the elderly goes the opposite way—often at a plummeting rate. You can make plans and strategize all you want, but you can't truly know what their needs will be until you're knee-deep in the process.

At first, taking care of Mama was simple. In fact, it was downright convenient. When she was going back and forth from Florida, I could make sure she got to the routine doctor and dentist appointments she'd neglected all those years (can't say I was surprised), and I could get her alternative treatments such as acupuncture and Chinese herbs. Sure, she was horrible at taking care of herself, but in the early days, her care was a bit easier to micromanage. If I could just stay one step ahead—checking on her, making sure she got to her appointments, and monitoring her overall health—I could prevent things from going downhill too fast.

Or so I thought.

Every week, a man named Michael came over to give Mama craniosacral therapy. One day, he called me and told me he couldn't get her on the massage table because she was in too much pain. Finally, she confided to him that she'd fallen in the bathtub but didn't want to tell anyone because she didn't want to inconvenience us. She'd broken four ribs.

Now, I've had a bruised rib before, and I can tell you for a fact it's *excruciating*, to the point where wearing a seatbelt is unbearable. But, like always, Mama never complained. She never let on that she was in pain. But I could hear it in her voice, in the way she breathed while sitting on the sofa or walking up the stairs.

At that time, she was still going back and forth from North Carolina, but after a return trip in 2001, we noticed she seemed kind of lethargic. Thankfully, I'd scheduled her a physical, and when the doctor finally got the blood work, he called me and told me to drive her to the hospital immediately because she was anemic and losing blood from somewhere inside her body. A colonoscopy revealed she had cancer, and they had to remove half her colon.

As they wheeled her away to emergency surgery, she smiled and sang her trademark hymn: "*Why worry when you can pray? Why worry when you can pray . . .*"

I just stood there and bawled. Ultimately, the surgery went well, and she made a remarkable recovery. Luckily, she didn't need chemotherapy or radiation. But this marked a major turning point in our relationship—or, at least, a major realization on my part. I couldn't trust my agreeable, considerate mother to call on me when something was wrong. All the money and medical resources in the world wouldn't fix that problem. I didn't just have to take care of her, I also had to *monitor* her. It was frustrating that she wouldn't tell me when she needed help, but bless her heart, she didn't want to be a burden and didn't understand that this made it more difficult to care for her.

Then came the headaches. Mama began getting them frequently, practically living on painkillers just to get through the day, and an MRI revealed numerous lesions on her brain. On top of being treated for skin cancer, she went in so the doctors could assess these areas, and finally, the neurologist recommended surgery to remove one of the tumors. During the recovery, I moved her in with us for six months so I could take care of her. But she made it clear she didn't want it to be permanent. She didn't want to be a burden. We ended up getting her a little condo across the street from the ocean. It was ten minutes from our house, so we could easily go back and forth.

My mama loved the beach. In spite of my son Gray's lessons, she couldn't swim a lick, and she nearly drowned in the ocean after being sucked into the undertow. But she didn't let that deter her love for the water. Despite the swimming hazard, her little apartment seemed to be the perfect solution, something small and simple where I could pop in on her and she could be happy and relatively independent. But like I said, aging isn't just physical. It was around this time we started seeing the real, telltale signs of the changes happening in Mama's mind.

We truly understand so little about the brain. Physical symptoms are relatively easy to identify, but things get a lot stickier when it comes to the aging mind. What's the difference between honest forgetfulness and the early stages of Alzheimer's? We've all spent a frustrating amount of time searching for our misplaced car keys, and I've lost track of how many instances I've walked into a room, only to forget what I meant to do there in the first place. Hair grays and skin wrinkles, but how are you supposed to tell when someone's own brain begins to turn on them? How are you supposed to protect them from an illness they don't even realize they have?

Mama had always been a busy person. She was constantly losing and misplacing things, bustling around like a whirlwind as she picked away at her never-ending to-do list. Between the frenzy of work, raising kids, and taking care of *everyone else* around her, it wasn't uncommon for her glasses or the car keys to end up somewhere they didn't belong. She had everything on her mind all the time, and for all her heart and kindness, she never was much of an organizer. (All those genes must have passed straight to me.) So when things began going missing in her condo, I initially didn't think too much of it.

Then I realized things weren't just misplaced or abandoned. Mama was purposefully hiding them. Little items from around the house would be gone for days, and I would find them in the washing machine or the dryer. All of a sudden, it seemed like a good chunk of our time together involved searching for a lost something or another.

I always tried to be patient with her. I never wanted to demean or embarrass her. I wasn't sure how much she understood about what she was doing, so I had to broach the subject delicately.

"Mom," I'd ask when this or that went missing, "where do you think you put it?"

Her response was like a broken record. I think she was beginning to realize what was happening but didn't want to let on that her mind wasn't what it used to be. On top of dealing with the pressure of the brain lesions, her moments of clarity seemed to be getting more jarring. She would crack a big smile and say, "I think a little gremlin got it."

And then she'd laugh.

Alzheimer's is a slow thing, more of a fade than a diagnosis. There's no real way to track where someone's at in the process. Oftentimes, *they* don't even know how much they've lost.

Eventually, the blame shifted from the impish little gremlin to more sinister explanations like burglary and theft. Suspicion turned to hunches, which then grew into full-fledged paranoia. Whenever something went missing, she became convinced that someone had broken into her apartment and stolen it. It wasn't that the item was misplaced; she was *unsafe*.

These theories must have been easier for her to accept. When you can't trust your own mind, how can you trust anyone? Is it easier to accept that you're the one responsible for something you don't remember doing? Or that someone else—something beyond your control, outside your own body—is plotting against you?

We know that scapegoating, as silly and irrational as it may be, can be simpler than facing the truth. Humans have been doing it for thousands of years. Of course, my mother felt unsafe. Her fears and feelings of vulnerability were very real and by no means unfounded. But the threat to her health and livelihood wasn't from the outside. It came from the *inside*. In many ways, that was worse.

For the first time in my life, I saw Mama getting scared. She'd always been able to care for others and pull herself through anything, even when she didn't have two nickels to rub together. She'd chased off hoochie-coochie girls, survived multiple bouts with cancer, come out of brain surgery, and lived to see her great-grandchildren off to school. But this was something she couldn't muscle her way through. She couldn't just suffer in silence. Little by little, the layers of her identity began falling away. It was only natural for her to cling to anything that felt safe or familiar—things that made her feel more like herself. "I don't have money," she kept telling me and my husband. "I need to get a job."

This was completely ridiculous, and part of her must have known that. She was over eighty years old, and she'd been retired for decades. But at that point, she seemed to be desperately hanging on to anything she could. Working was something that made her feel seen, a way to get out and participate as a contributing member of society. I had my own children, and they had children of their own. We didn't need her in the way she was used to being needed. That must have stripped her down to her core.

She was nothing but gracious to Gregg, but she also couldn't stand the fact that he was taking care of her. Eventually, we started coming up with little white lies of our own, telling her that the cash in her wallet was money she'd made or that she owned the apartment she was staying in. At holidays and family meals, she would get more and more agitated if there was nothing for her to do. "Just let me do the dishes," she would say, a thin note of desperation in her voice. "Please, just let me do *something*."

Every time she wanted to do something or go somewhere like she used to, all I could see was danger. But from her perspective, it must have looked like we were chipping away at her independence.

When my dad died, we brought his Lincoln Continental down to Florida so Mama would have a car. In a scalding twist of irony, she got to drive the one vehicle he never let her touch. Thank God she was mostly on the A1A and the little side streets around our community. I was a nervous wreck just knowing she was at the wheel.

It wasn't about the driving. It had never been about the driving. It was about her independence, the ability to go wherever she wanted whenever she wanted. And later, around the same time we took her driver's license away, we had to confiscate her pocketbook as well. She loved my husband dearly, but I could see the grief in her eyes when she shook her finger at him. Jokingly, of course. She never *actually* rebelled. But that didn't mean it wasn't a real and painful loss.

"That's the only thing I have." She would cry, and the frailty in her voice broke my heart. Sure, she had me. Sure, she had her extended family. But she wasn't upset with the life I'd built for her in Florida or even the way I'd incorporated her into my own. She was mourning the lost pieces of herself. When she became physically and mentally unable to live the life she'd lived for so long, she was adrift.

We sent her home to North Carolina to visit her family, knowing it was probably the last time she would see her sister Helen, whose health was also declining. The beginning of the trip went well enough, but on the way back, she forgot where she was and had an episode, terrified that the airline stewards "wouldn't let her off the bus." By the time we got her back home, her mind was even worse. The world around her was rapidly changing—her body and her own *existence* was rapidly changing—and she had no idea what to do.

It was hard to watch. Here was this woman, who'd given so much to me, living in so much pain, and I didn't know how to make it better. I was still juggling my own life and my own family as I tried my best to help her navigate her situation. It felt like a never-ending balancing act. No matter where and how I spent my time, it wasn't enough. Sure, Mama was physically healthy for her age (in my opinion, the alternative treatments and Chinese herbs made all the difference), but she still didn't want to bother anyone when she was lonely or feeling under the weather. I would check in with her every day, asking about how she was and if anything was wrong. But I knew she wouldn't answer honestly. And we were getting to the point where that could get dangerous.

We decided to buy her a condo in an assisted living community, hoping it would help ease her loneliness and provide the facilities she needed. With Gregg being in the health-care business, we made sure to find the best of the best for her, a top-rated place in Delray Beach. The facility was gorgeous, but we soon discovered that the company of the other residents made for a bad fit. The other tenants came from high-society, old money that came with its own distinct culture. Mama had never been part of that world. She almost never had her hair teased and done like most women in her era did weekly. She had never had a manicure or pedicure. When I offered these to her when she moved to Florida, she quickly responded, "I thought that was only for poodles." What made things even worse for her ability to assimilate at this facility was that she'd never had a heart for bridge—the "coin of the realm" when it came to the social hierarchy. These people already had their inner circles, and none of them were quick to welcome the woman from rural

North Carolina, especially one whose mind was deteriorating. There was one kind lady who consistently joined her for lunch, but there's nothing quite like feeling alone in a sea of people. I guess Mama's sister was right after all—this was not a "grits and collards" kind of place. I still stand by my decision to move her down to Florida, but of course there were, and always are, I suppose, complexities.

Still, Mama loved her little place by the water, especially her access to the community pool. Then another grumpy resident scolded her for not wearing the right type of robe on the pool deck, and that was that. She was too scared and timid to go down there anymore, terrified of breaking another rule. No matter how much care we took to find a nice residency, there wasn't a lot we could do about the other residents. None of these places would ever feel like home.

One day, she took off on a walk down the beach, angry at us when we told her she shouldn't be walking alone. Eventually, a man spotted her and called the police. She was five miles away from her apartment, completely alone with no idea where she was or how she'd gotten there. "I knew what I was doing," she said. "I was just taking a walk."

But I knew better. As much as it was a relief to find her safe and sound, the knot in my gut only cinched tighter. She was losing things, wandering off, and nearly caught her apartment on fire one day trying to warm something up in the microwave. She finally stopped going to the dining rooms to eat, and every time I visited her, she looked a little frailer and a little more confused. Even when I brought her food, there was no way to ensure she was eating it.

You could hire staff from the facility to help you take care of your loved one, but the attendants rotated, sending a new person every day. I understand this was just the work schedule, but for someone struggling with dementia, it's like waking up each day with a brand-new hair color. These caretakers would be in charge of bathing and grooming her, which became more of an ordeal the worse she got. My mama never had a bad thing to say about anyone. But something came out of her as her mind went, and I can only describe it as repressed anger. She hated it when the women would come to help her shower. She would get visibly agitated and upset, which wasn't at all like her.

"My daddy's gonna kill you," she would warn the attendants. I wasn't sure if something had happened to her or if she was just uncomfortable with being touched so intimately by a stranger. But bless her heart, she had to be clean. They didn't have a choice.

Mama wasn't just having trouble remembering, she was also deeply lonely. I spent as much time with her as I could between my own family responsibilities and health issues, but I wasn't my daddy. I couldn't be the companion she so desperately missed.

A dear friend of mine had a daughter with a heart for the elderly. Her name was Kim, and she was a kind and attentive caretaker. We hired her to spend time with Mama when I couldn't be there, but one day, she called me in tears.

She had found Mama in the bathroom, curled up on the floor in a fetal position. The image still breaks my heart. This was my beautiful, elegant mother, scared and all alone.

This was the last straw. Something had to be done—something different, maybe even drastic. And it was there and then I decided I would go to the ends of the earth to find a solution. If Mama was going to live in a place where she was comfortable, I was going to have to find her full-time care.

Thus began the process of trying to find the right person. We got Mama another little apartment two minutes down the street from us, a tiny little place where she could see the ocean while sitting on her couch. I started working with several agencies, and they sent person after person to interview for the job.

"We're sending our best," they would always tell me. But that was a big, fat lie. I quickly learn these companies never send their best. They simply send whoever's *available*. We set up cameras in the room to assess each one, and none of them took the time or the effort to properly care for Mama. At this point, she was also deteriorating into Alzheimer's, and routine was everything when it came to keeping her feeling grounded and safe. The influx of different workers every day was disastrous, just as bad as the assisted living home. She didn't recognize anyone and had no idea what to expect from day to day. And, in her defense, neither did we.

I was exasperated by the process. Exhausted, deflated, and bizarrely lonely. It was the first time the truth of the matter really hit me—my mother wasn't my mother anymore. Not in the sense I'd known her as a mother, anyway. In a strange, surreal way, I felt orphaned. The two people who'd taken care of me since my birth were both gone. Mama wasn't the woman I remembered. She was the child I'd never known.

Before she came down with dementia, she would often say to me, "Marsha, I think I'm the only one who worries about you."

Weirdly enough, I took comfort in that. No matter how tired or frazzled I got, somebody would have me on their mind and in their heart. But now, it was my turn to worry about Mama. Our roles were changing in ways I could have never imagined.

This was also when Mama started to get scared. Truly, deeply scared. On particularly bad nights, she would lie awake, terrified, weeping like a little girl for her mom and dad. She didn't remember where she was. She didn't remember where they'd gone. My mama, the woman who'd walked into a pitch-black church without any fear, the woman I'd depended on my whole life, was gone long before she died.

After weeks and weeks of dealing with the agencies and interviewing caretaker after caretaker, I confided my frustration to a man who worked at the local tennis club. He loved Mama dearly and often let her eat her meals there, even though she wasn't a member. The club itself had many elderly members, so he sniffed around and got back to me with a couple names.

"Call Sarah first," he told me. "She's supposed to be the best."

And he was right. When Sarah came to meet with us, we knew she would be a great fit. Later, we met Sarah's sister, Regina, and she fell in love with Mama as well—so much so that we convinced her to move down from Canada to help take care of Mama. Regina was sunny and friendly, always one to keep her patients clean and beautiful, while Sarah was more clinical and focused on the technicalities of keeping them healthy. They were the team I'd been looking for. They would dance with Mama, sing with her, sleep with her, and even stay with her while she used the bathroom. She loved them so much, she refused to eat unless they ate with her.

For the first time in a long time, I felt like I could breathe.

I was lucky to find Sarah and Regina, lucky to have them and lucky to have the means to have them. I know full well my situation was a lot different than it is for most people. Because Gregg owned health-care facilities, we had access to a lot of resources most people don't. His businesses are known for having top-quality staff and taking exemplary care of their residents, but even having the best facilities and the most amazing workers doesn't address the complex situation of caring for an aging parent. Not everyone has time to look after their loved one. Not everyone has the skill or resources to accommodate for their various health conditions. Even with all the time, money, and access in the world, there's no simple solution.

Like I've said, I'm a planner. When my dad died, I knew I was going to be the one caring for Mama until the very end. But even years of planning couldn't have prepared me for doing the right thing, and maybe it's not about the *right* or *wrong* thing as much as is it about doing the best with what you've got.

These days, we face an unprecedented number of aging people who are living, on average, longer than ever before. You can't watch the Hallmark Channel for five minutes without seeing some sort of advertisement for antiaging this or that, and we openly talk about the face creams we use to prevent wrinkles or the workouts we do to fight back against our sagging skin.

That's the danger of taking the "us versus them" mentality when it comes to caring for seniors. We can fight against aging as much as we want, but do we actually have a *plan* for how we're going to take care of them? And someday, when we're in the same position, will we be wishing that someone else would take better care of us?

No matter how much I planned, I couldn't anticipate Mama's multidimensional needs as her dementia worsened into Alzheimer's and her health declined. I was in a fortunate situation—more fortunate than most—and I *still* struggled to meet her needs. It wasn't just a matter of keeping her clean and fed. Even those of us who have dogs and cats know there's a big difference between caring for something and simply keeping it alive. No, I wanted to do my best to ensure Mama was constantly in a place of respect and dignity, and even though I was able to hire private caretakers, it was extremely difficult.

Mama's case was also a special one. The reality most seniors face is losing their independence when their loved ones aren't able to care for them. It's a sad and ugly truth, but it's a situation our generation needs to talk about. Who cares for the elderly when they need constant care, when you have a job, a family, and responsibilities of your own? Who's going to not just take care of their physical needs, but also their emotional and psychological needs? And who's supposed to advocate for these patients when they can't even trust their own minds? Most of us don't like to think about having to live under supervision, but the idea of accommodating our elderly parents into our own busy lives is downright inconceivable.

These issues are sticky. They always have been. We love having funny grandpas or cute, cookie-baking grandmas, but as soon as it comes down to who's changing catheters or cleaning up messes, the responsibility becomes much less charming.

And these are just examples of physical symptoms. No one warned me about the hurt, anger, and frustration of taking away someone's freedoms—key parts of their identity—for their own safety. No one talks about comforting your terrified mother when she forgets herself and breaks down weeping like a child. It was more than humiliating; it was terrifying. Aging tore her apart piece by piece, mind, body, and soul; and there was nothing I could do but stand back and watch. We could take her car, her pocketbook, and even her microwave, but it was losing herself that broke her.

My mother was a caring, beautiful, and dignified woman all throughout her life. She deserved respect, and finding a way to afford her that respect while receiving the care she needed was a never-ending battle. I didn't just want her to be healthy; I wanted her to be *happy*, to live a full and joyous life all the way to the bitter end. After a lifetime of taking care of others, she deserved at least that much.

This isn't a fun subject to talk about. If anything, it's a subject people avoid. And it's not just because taking care of our elderly is complicated, political, or even daunting—it's because we know, deep down inside, that these will be the same discussions our children have about us. That's a scary thought, not something I regularly bring up at dinner parties or chatting in line at the grocery store. But birth and death are the two things every single human being have in common. Every second we live is a second we age, and if we refuse to think about our elderly and how we take care of them, our willful ignorance may very well come back to haunt us.

11

The Gentle Art of Grief

Most of us are familiar with the five stages of grief. These stages, or the Kübler-Ross model published by psychiatrist Elizabeth Kübler-Ross in her 1969 book *On Death and Dying*, are pretty much baked into our national psyche. At one time or another, we've probably all heard a reference to at least one of these stages: denial, anger, bargaining, depression, and acceptance.

Whether it's dealing with the death of a loved one or even losing a career, it's safe to say these steps are a fundamental part of every human experience. We lose something important to us, then we set off on the noble path to healing. We experience a major trauma, so we launch into a quest for meaning, to understand why this horrible thing happened, how it defines us, and how we can triumph through adversity.

On the surface, it seems pretty straightforward. Something bad happens, so you work through it and end up becoming a better person in the end. Sure, that's oversimplified, but for those who aren't dealing with complex emotions like grief, the process *has to be* oversimplified. Our friend loses their spouse, so we wait in anxious expectation until they're "ready" to love again. Our child loses a pet, so we buy them another in hopes they'll "get over it." We even make up silly rules like waiting half the length of a previous relationship before dating someone new after a breakup.

From this perspective, the cycle of grief seems clean. Digestible. Linear. But this is where we get everything wrong.

If you've ever experienced deep grief, you know the process isn't simple. For some, it may be linear, but for me, it's been anything but straightforward. Instead of a continuous line, it feels more like a wonky crochet pattern, crossing every which way and doubling back over itself. Modern professionals such as Dr. Sheila Clark are now proposing multidimensional grief models, more like waypoints on a map than a traceable line.* One day, you move from rejection to anger. The next, you travel to the isolation stage, but then take a hard swivel and find yourself back in good old rejection. There's no "set path," and there's no defining how long you stay in each stage—or even how many times you may revert back to it.

---

* Sheila Clark, "Mapping Grief: An Active Approach to Grief Resolution," *Death Studies* 25: 531–48, 2001.

The psychology runs deep, and there's not enough room in this book to go into it fully. The point is that grief may look different for everyone, but the process is *never* simple.

Take my parents, for instance. I was devastated when my father died. I'd always been a daddy's girl. His quiet strength and support meant everything to me. I related much more to him growing up than I did to my mother, who was always hustling around to be there for everyone else. Half the time, I was juggling conflicting feelings of yearning for her attention and being awestruck by her genuine care for every person in her life. The other half, I was wrestling with feeling less-than for not being able to live up to her motherly example. She was a genuine saint.

My parents were two very different people who died in two very different ways. It's not completely right to say that losing Mama was harder than losing Daddy. "Harder" just isn't accurate. "Different" is probably the better word for it. I didn't take care of my daddy at the end of his life like I did for Mama. He wasn't completely dependent on me. Even though Mama was old and frail, Daddy's death was a bit easier to swallow. Taking care of someone implies responsibility, even if it's unspoken, unfair, or undefined. There's still a part of me that feels like I failed her.

Maybe that's selfish. Maybe that's short-sighted. But shock, guilt, shame, and even a crisis of values are all waypoints on Dr. Clark's grief map. You don't travel them in a straight line. You ping-pong back and forth until you're sure your head will explode.

Grief isn't simple, linear, or even explainable. It's not something you can define or plan for, which is probably why it's been so difficult for me. Grief isn't a science, it's an *art*. And like any form of art, it requires gentleness, both with yourself and with others.

This book isn't about blame, but that doesn't mean I don't struggle with those feelings. I don't speak with our family doctor, Sarah, or Harriet anymore. Every time I think about them in anger or bitterness, those feelings reflect right back onto my own guilt. After all, the ones who judge others harshly tend to judge themselves the same way. I can hear my mama right now saying, "You can hate the sin but not the sinner."

I can sit here and blame anyone and everyone for the way things happened, but at the end of the day, the only motivations I can honestly critique are my own. I'm still tearing myself up over all those stupid rules. Was I really trying to protect Mama by not going in to see her on that final day? Or was I just working to protect myself? Am I truly any better than the people who disappointed me? Or was it just an unprecedented and complex time where we all had hard decisions to make, even Sarah and Harriet?

Grief is complicated like that. The journey is different for every person, and while we can share our experiences and help each other heal (that's my ultimate hope by writing this book), in the thick of things, nothing feels lonelier. Of course, my children are wonderful. From the boys coming out to visit Mama in her apartment to Brittany sacrificing so much to take care of her, to Lauren not coming in an attempt to protect Mama, I couldn't ask for more selfless and caring kids. They loved their Grandma Gray; it warms my heart to think about how much they honored her both throughout and after her passing.

Still, their love for Mama isn't the same as mine. It can't be. No one had the same kind of relationship with her.

It's crazy how you can feel so alone even when surrounded by loving, genuine people. Of course, Mama's sisters mourned. My brother mourned, and so did my children and *their* children. Seeing Mama's great-grandbabies at her memorial was bittersweet, joyful because they so clearly loved her and missed her, but sad because even then, I knew their grief processes were going to look much different than mine.

My fourteen grandchildren were so young. Of course, they were sad, but they didn't understand the depth of grief I was feeling—and to be honest, am still wading through at my own tired pace. But how could I ever expect that from them? How could anyone understand what it was like to hold Mama's hand when she was weeping, terrified, and crying out for her own dead parents?

My children were (and continue to be) busy with their own lives. That's a wonderful and beautiful thing. I can never know the true measure of their own grief, but life has a funny way of chugging along regardless. Time moves so fast, even when it's moving through sadness. Hours melt into days, days melt into months, and all of a sudden, you realize you have to be "normal" again—at least on the outside. Kids need to get to school. Bills have to be paid. Soccer games are still on the schedule, and everyone is still going to be asking what we're all doing for Thanksgiving.

Life moves on with or without you. It's not about fairness. It just is what it is. One moment, the grandkids are sniffling along with me because they sense, even when they don't quite understand, that Great Nine is gone. Maybe the younger ones aren't old enough to wrap their heads around the permanence of death, but they can still *feel* the loss. One of our grandchildren developed major separation anxiety soon after Mama's death and a fear that his parents were going to die. Great Nine's death, and COVID in general, certainly affected his sensitive psyche at a critical age.

However, the next moment, there are bubbles or toys or someone splashing in the pool, and their attention is completely diverted. They're off to the next thing, learning, growing, and living life, while I'm left in the depths of grief. Part of me feels guilty for that, like I should be stronger, but I can't just "get over it." And I don't think I should. The process takes as long as it takes. There's nothing you can do to sidestep or avoid it; you can only work through it.

Life seems to move much faster for my kids—and even faster for my grandkids. That can feel lonely and isolating, but I'm also learning to look at it from a softer perspective. My whole life, I've pushed to do everything for my children. Now they're doing the same thing for their own little ones, and with every generation, that looks a little different.

When I think about the loneliness of grief, I can't help but think about Mama. How many times was she alone in the midst of sadness, losing her parents, her husband, her childhood friends—even Miriam, the elderly woman who became her "baby" while she was living in Florida? And how many times did I fly right by her, pressing on in my own rhythm of daily life? She must have felt just as isolated and misunderstood as I do. But how could I possibly have understood that?

These thoughts bring sadness, but also grace and compassion for my own family and for myself. If grief were linear, it would be much easier. There would be a simple way forward, and we could help each other, even if that meant crawling along inch by inch.

But grief isn't linear. It isn't circular, square, or even three-dimensional. I don't have to harbor any disappointment that the rest of my family doesn't feel the same way I do, and I don't have to feel guilty that my own mourning process has been so long and painful. When we start seeing grief for what it is instead of what we think it should be, we start to find *grace*—grace for others, grace for ourselves, and grace for the difference in our processes.

This is why grief is an art, not a science. We have guidelines, not rules. We have waypoints, but no clearly prescribed path. Working through any loss, no matter how large or how small, is completely personal—a brand-new venture into a deep, dark forest that looks different every time you enter. As scary as that seems, it's also a relief. There's no right or wrong way to let go. Your process doesn't have to look like anyone else's.

There's grace in the art of grief, and there also has to be a great amount of gentleness. Gentleness for ourselves, gentleness for others, and gentleness for the journey—whatever that may look like.

12

My Baby

When my mama became helpless, something strange and unexpected happened. Of course, I expected her to get frailer. I expected her health to go downhill. But I didn't expect to get so close to her in her final days.

Things were different with my dad. He had my mom to take care of him as his condition worsened, and his mind was as sharp as it had ever been. When Daddy died, I lost the man I'd known my whole life. He was the same person I remembered from my childhood, brave and strong in his own quiet way.

Things weren't the same with Mama.

Your relationship with your parents is always shifting. It shifts when you start developing independence. It shifts when you become a teenager and criticize every little thing they do. It shifts when you get married and go off to start a life of your own, when you have children, and in thousands of other small, beautiful ways that come and go with the seasons of life. For me, the most jarring shift was becoming my mother's caretaker. As her health declined and she went from not knowing where she was to being completely unable to feed herself, our relationship deepened in a way I still can't explain. It was more like the care of a young child than an adult woman. She was so fragile and helpless. I felt like I was taking care of a baby.

But not just a baby. *My* baby. Our spirits were connected in such a unique and powerful way. Taking care of Mama in those final years was the first time I ever truly felt a soul bond with her. There were so many threads between us I'd never felt before—our family, what we'd seen, and where we'd come from. This deep, almost spiritual sense of compassion and connection was what I had longed for my whole life.

Of course, I love my kids more than anything in this world. But when they were babies, I didn't have an entire life's history with them. They were helpless and completely dependent on me, but I didn't have memories of them tending to my scrapes and bruises or staying up late in the night to make treats for my elementary classroom.

I don't have clear memories of Mama taking care of me as a baby either. I assume most of us don't remember that far back. As we go about living our daily lives, we don't often pause to think about just how much our parents cared for us. But when Mama reverted and suddenly those roles reversed, we bonded in a way I never could have expected.

In 2008, Brad Pitt starred in a movie of the same name based on F. Scott Fitzgerald's short story "The Curious Case of Benjamin Button." For those who haven't seen the movie (no spoilers, I promise), the premise is simple enough: Benjamin Button is a young man growing up in the 1860s, though "growing up" isn't quite accurate. He's born looking like a seventy-year-old man, and he ages in reverse, steadily "growing" backward until his final days as a baby.

It's a crazy concept, but maybe not as bizarre as it first seems. Mama started developing dementia when I began wrestling through my own health issues. At one point, I didn't leave my house for nearly six months. I was longing for a parent, for Mama to comfort me and take care of me like she did when I was a child. She was still mostly independent, but all the logistics—food, lodging, and medical care—were up to me. I made sure she had groceries, that the rent and utilities were paid, and that she had transportation wherever she needed to go. If she had food in the fridge, she could prepare a meal for herself. It felt like caring for a teenager, someone preoccupied with self-sufficiency while lacking the means to provide for themselves.

Then she really started slipping, and the reversion got even worse. Like a child, she had to have someone looking after her all hours of the day to make sure she didn't end up hurt or catching something on fire. I was adamant about staying home with my children when they were young, but all of a sudden, I was dealing with frantic worries about keeping my mother supervised. Was she truly being taken care of? If I trusted someone else to watch her, was I risking her being abused? If she was in a group home, what happened when she was unhappy or didn't get along with the other residents? In a lot of ways, I was just as frazzled as I was when raising my own kids.

Even with all the parenting books available these days, nobody has the same experience. There's no official manual for raising a child. Every kid is completely different, and no amount of research can prepare you for what life ends up throwing your way. At the end of the day, you hope that every parent is simply doing their best.

That should be comforting, but when I was taking care of Mama, it was also extremely frustrating. My heart knew I needed to let it go, accept I was doing my best, and give the rest to God, but my brain (as always) was trying to out-plan any hypothetical obstacle. I was always on guard, hypertense and ready to grab the phone as soon as it rang. As her dementia got worse, she would often faint randomly. Someone would call her an ambulance, and I would rush to the ER, only to find her up and laughing like a child, completely oblivious to what had happened.

There was no telling how to gauge anything. She didn't communicate how far gone she was, but that wasn't her fault either. Whether it was hiding her broken ribs from us, being unable to articulate how bad things actually were, or even just forgetting, it was like trying to coax out symptoms from a child.

"Where does it hurt?"

"Do you remember what happened?"

"What's the last thing you remember?"

Her body aged one way, but her mind seemed to go in the complete opposite direction. She went from laughing and crying like a child, weeping for her parents when she woke up late at night, to not registering much at all. We had to feed her, bathe her, dress her, and do her hair. I feel horrible admitting that, sometimes, when she was having a particularly bad day or struggling a lot, my mind went to a dark place. I started wondering if the struggle was even worth it.

This wasn't because I wanted to lose her. I just couldn't take seeing her the way she was; it was heart-wrenching. There were days I would leave her apartment sobbing, begging God to call her home because her quality of life had gotten so bad. She was scared and confused, more vulnerable than I'd ever seen her. She wasn't the strong, confident woman I remembered. In a lot of ways, she was already gone.

I know. It's awful. It was so painful to watch. Mama couldn't communicate to me how she was feeling, couldn't let me know when she was ready to move on from her tired body. How can anyone be completely sure about a choice like that in the first place? We didn't know—I don't think she knew, for that matter—so we did the best we could.

When I think about Mama as my baby, how much I cared for her and how she depended on me, it brings back the bittersweetness of those final days in early May 2020. There are a lot of emotions surrounding that week, especially when I remember how hard I fought to get what I thought would be simple things for Mama: antibiotics, oxygen, and even hospice care. There's still deep anger and betrayal. These memories sting years later, partially because of those who couldn't and some who didn't do their jobs, and partially because I feel like I failed to do mine.

But there are tender moments in these memories, too, particularly around those who were there for Mama—Javier, Regina, Brittany, and the rest of my family. When we knew Mama was dying and everybody started rushing to see her, it almost felt like gathering to see a new baby. Hello and goodbye may be different words with completely different meanings, but for a lot of people, the first and last of these take place in the same place—a hospital room. A bed surrounded by loved ones.

I'm a firm believer in the power of touch. There's God-given power in the palm of your hand and laying hands on someone has always been a staple of Christian tradition. This may sound like a lot of hooey to people who don't practice the same faith, but science has been catching up to why these traditions have existed for so long. Doctors try to get skin-to-skin contact between mother and child as soon as they can after the baby is born because that physical touch is so important. It's comforting, and as the child grows to recognize themselves as an individual, the child constantly looks back to that caregiver's touch for protection and reassurance.

If you've ever spent time around infants, you know that their sense of touch is one of the first faculties to develop. Touch a baby's hand, and their palm will close. Touch the bottoms of their feet, and their little toes will curl. Grabbing something and holding on is one of our first instincts.

Is it any wonder why it's so important for the elderly? If hospital volunteers are recruited to hold, rock, and soothe babies, why aren't we looking at the importance of physical touch for elderly patients?

When I first saw Mama interacting with her caretaker Regina, I knew we'd found a wonderful match. Regina was always hands-on with Mama, hugging her, cuddling with her, and holding her hand. My mother had always been openly affectionate, but as the other parts of her mind fell away, she would cling to you like a life raft in a storm. In the days leading up to her death, I remember getting a message from Regina: *"I will hold her all night. She knows I am here. I asked her if she wanted me to sleep with her, and she nodded."*

In the past, I'd never been much of a touchy-feely person when it came to my mother. I took for granted that she was always there, my mama as I'd known her for so many years. But then she became my baby, and all that changed. When we were still quarantining and I was visiting her from outside the screen door of her little apartment, all I wanted in the whole world was to touch her, to hold her in my arms and kiss her face as I sang to her. It was torturous to see her like that, my baby gasping and struggling to breathe as I stood by, helpless, watching. It tore a hole in me from the inside out. I would stand at the door, talking to her, singing to her through the screen or over the phone—anything to let her know I was there.

That's a different kind of helplessness, a vulnerability that haunts my dreams. Once in a while, I'll wake up in a cold sweat, breathless from horrible nightmares about not being able to get milk or medicine for my children. That fear of being unable to provide for my children is primal, and it ties right back to struggling to take care of Mama at the end of her life.

Before I got the COVID results, I was right by her side every day, crying in her face, holding her hand, and singing. But when the tests came back positive (one day before she died), all that changed. Part of it was fear. Part of it was conflicting guidance. But FaceTiming and singing to her through the door to her apartment just wasn't the same. I can't say whether that decision was right or wrong. It just was what it was. I have made my peace with this because Mama knew I wasn't good in situations involving death, needles, or medical interventions. She wouldn't have wanted me to be so uncomfortable. Yes, she was always thinking of others way before herself. She and I were bonded, mother and child, closer than I'd ever felt in my whole life. I'd once been her baby, and now she was mine.

I can't imagine how new parents handled birthing during the time of COVID. Being unable to have your loved ones with you during that important moment, unable to visit the newborn or the mother must have left so many feeling lost and isolated during what should have been one of the most joyful moments of their lives. *I* was frustrated having to stay away from Mama when she was struggling so much, and I nearly lost my head trying to micromanage everything from afar.

At 5:45 a.m., on Wednesday, May 6, we finally got our COVID tests back. I was positive, and so were Mama and Regina. Sarah and Javier, thankfully, were negative. Regina started freaking out, not for herself or her new husband (who would end up contracting the virus from her and nearly dying in the hospital), but for Mama.

Sarah called in to tell us she wasn't coming in to relieve her sister. She told Regina she was crazy for staying on. But as scared as Regina was, that made her angry. "This is your calling," she told her sister. "How can you do this to someone you've worked for so many years?"

She was frightened. Sarah was frightened. We were all frightened. This isn't a place to be angry or pass judgment on what someone did or didn't do. I'm just grateful Regina did stay on to help us, that she and Javier took such painstaking care of Mama despite the personal risk.

By that time, my daughter Brittany had arrived. I could finally let my guard down and catch my breath. Here was somebody I trusted implicitly. Finally, I had a partner, someone I knew would be there no matter what. That gave me comfort beyond measure.

Brittany and Regina administered the morphine, and for the first time in a long time, Mama looked peaceful. She was no longer struggling to breathe. We once again got creative. We FaceTimed with Regina's daughter in Canada who is a nurse who specializes in geriatrics. She looked at Mama and did an assessment. Brittany mentioned how helpful this phone call was. Although Brittany went to PA school and takes care of patients with cancer, she felt helpless when it came to the death and dying process and keeping patients comfortable as they passed. Regina's daughter had an expertise and insight that put everyone's mind at ease in those final hours.

"Any minute," Brittany kept saying. "Any minute."

I had a long talk with my mother that day, recalling everything I'd done in the last week and how hard I'd fought to save her. I don't know why I felt like I had to apologize, to justify my actions and my decisions. I guess it was because, even after all that had happened, I still felt guilty that I hadn't done enough for her. Everyone was advising me to stay away from Mama, and the fact that I listened is one of my biggest regrets. I already knew I had COVID. What was the point?

I was also at the brink of exhaustion. The head of my husband's nursing staff was getting concerned, telling me I needed to rest and get off my feet. But for all my careful planning, there was still so much to do. I contacted a Baptist chaplain to talk with Mama via phone and comfort her. My brother, Eddie, and his family were driving through the night to get to Mama before she died, so there was lodging and accommodations to assist with. Our house was a no-go—not when half of us were infected—and most hotels were closed. It was a storm of phone calls, arrangements, and pending grief, but thankfully, Mama's medicines were kicking in. At least I could take comfort in the fact that she was comfortable. Even if I couldn't hold my baby, it was enough to know that she was safe and in good hands.

As horrible as it all sounds, we got creative and did everything we could, considering the circumstances, to express our love and to be there for her as she passed. We did a lot of FaceTiming, singing, playing gospel music, reading Bible verses, praying, and holding her hand. We surrounded her with beautiful hand-made posters that the great grandchildren had crafted. We opened the door to let in the sunshine. We thanked her for the impact she had made on all of our lives. We did everything in our power to make her as comfortable as possible. It wasn't perfect, but it was as perfect as it could be at that particular time. I have to keep reminding myself of this to stay afloat.

Still, I can't stop feeling like I should have been there, holding her while she died. For my family, having someone there (preferably a close relative) in those last moments is a big deal. You need to be with your loved one when they pass on. You need to be touching them, comforting them right up to the end. We were all wearing N95 masks and wearing gloves. This must have been so confusing and even frightening for Mama. To this day, I can't say why I stayed away that last day. Maybe it was fear. Maybe it was exhaustion or decision overwhelm after sleepless nights and day after day of fighting. But I wasn't with my mother, my baby, when she died. I was cuddled up with Gregg in a twin bed, sweating through the air-conditionedless night. But when the moment came, it hit me hard, as clear and real as anything I've ever experienced.

I knew Mama was gone before I got the call from Regina. I woke up in the middle of the night knowing it was time, *feeling* her reluctance, as if she were hesitant to leave without knowing I would be okay. I've only had that level of intuition with my own children. Yes, she was ready to go. But she also needed me to let her go, to let her know that everything was going to be okay. Even in the midst of her pain and confusion, she was still worried about me. She was still my mama.

Thank you, God, I wrote. *Thank you for taking care of me, Regina, her husband, Gregg, Brittany, the boys . . . everybody who came to see Mama and all the heroes who were with her.*

Then my entry changed. I started writing directly to Mama. *I know that Jesus welcomed you with loving arms. You no longer have to worry about a thing. Your whole life, you were always worried for others, worried about bills, jobs, food . . . helping others. It's your time, Mama. Have a blast and dance without worrying, safe in Jesus's arms. I'll see you one day. I love you.*

My precious baby had finally moved on. But as comforting as it was to imagine her dancing free of fear and worry, it didn't help the heart-wrenching pain of loss.

There was still work to be done. I'd put in quite a bit of preparation in the previous years, planning for the inevitable, but there are some arrangements you just can't prepare for, decisions that had to be made in the moment.

My brother and his family drove all through the night to see Mama. He battles with his own health complications, so he never made it in her room. He talked to her from outside the door, though, and even though we were

Beach Babe

The Southwind

*Gregg, Mama's Firstborn
Grandson, and Our
Burgeoning Tennis Star*

Drew and Grandmama's Garden

New Lincoln Continental for Granddaddy

The Famous Sisters

*Pete and Adaline's
Fiftieth Wedding
Anniversary*

Gray Teaching Grandmama How to Swim

Mama Speaking at Cragmont

Mama Visiting Her Birth Home

Mama with Marsha and Eddie

Mama's Favorite Pastime, Singing Hymns with the Family

Our Team Mascot and Team Mama

*Brittany Chose Her Grandmama as Her Coater
in Her White Coat Ceremony*

Happy Times,
Fourth of July

Singing with Drew at the Piano

Mama Rejoicing at Christmas

The Beach and Chocolate-Covered Cherries, Mama's Favorites

Mama and Her Son

*Marsha Made Sure Mama
Had Her Biscuits*

Confused, But Always Loving Our Family Gatherings

Mama and Regina

A Special Bond Between Mama and Gregg

My Mama, My Baby

*Mama with Her
Drink of Choice,
Pepsi-Cola*

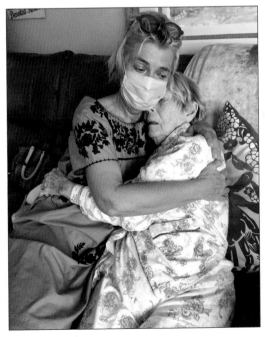

Hard Times

*Brittany Caring for Her
Grandmama*

Remembering Great Nine at the Beach

Adaline's Adventure Area Dedication, Cragmont

Eddie's Family

Marsha's Family

COVID positive at my house, he was able to stay at a local hotel. His daughter is a nurse, and at that time, only essential workers were even allowed to stay in hotels. He was there in that strange room when I called him to give him the news that Mama had passed. I can't imagine how lonely that must have felt for him.

Brittany decided to stay on and help, sorting through Mama's medications and cleaning out her fridge. She lived in our guest house to quarantine for another two weeks, and we fed her like a dog. I would put food outside the door, and she would come out and pick it up. We shared meals together from all the way across the yard. She pumped breast milk every few hours so that she could take it back to her young son. Mother's Day was three days after Mama passed, which made it even more gut-wrenching.

It was a good thing she did end up staying. Typically, when a patient dies, a hospice nurse confirms the death. We never had a hospice nurse due to COVID protocols. Remember, morphine was dropped off at Mama's door. Therefore Brittany ended up having to declare her own grandmama dead.

We had to do something with the body, though. Even though the hospice workers had not come, they sent a chaplain to meet us in the parking lot who read a few Bible verses while a local funeral home took care of Mama's remains. This was a real old-timey place, a place that sent professionals in suits who handled the situation with more care and reverence than I've ever seen before. We stood at a distance in the parking lot and watched as they carried

Mama's body out of her apartment and into the waiting hearse. In their dapper suits with their soft, kind mannerism, the funeral workers seemed almost out-of-place in our post-apocalyptic COVID world.

It was a relief to see them treat her so respectfully and attentively. It was the very least she deserved. That's not to say it wasn't hard to watch them take her away. After all those times riding with my daddy to take her to work or driving her and my kids back and forth from Florida, it was painful to think that total strangers would be taking her on one of her last rides.

Like I said, being physically "in-touch" with the dying is a big deal with my family. We come from old-fashioned stock, the kind of people who love a good funeral, especially when it involves open caskets and touching the bodies. I was never comfortable with that as a little girl, but I still understood how important the tradition was.

When Mama's sisters started calling, the first thing they asked was, "Were you with her?"

It wasn't about how she died. We didn't talk about how I fought so hard and so long to get her oxygen, medicine, caretakers, nurses, or even morphine. They explicitly wanted to know if I was there, holding her hand, when she breathed her last breath.

Of course, I don't think Mama's sisters meant this as a personal attack. But with all the guilt welling up, all the *couldas, shouldas, wouldas* already gnawing at the back of my brain like hungry woodlice, all I could think was, *You did it wrong. Everything you did was wrong. You were wrong not to be there. Wrong not to stay with her. Wrong to trust the wrong people. Wrong, wrong, wrong . . .*

There's a lot of talk about "mom guilt" these days, mothers who feel like no matter what they do or how they care for their children, they can't measure up to the insta-perfect, filtered images of modern parenting. You would think that with age and experience, these crushing feelings of guilt and inferiority would go away by the time you have to take care of an elderly parent. But they don't. If anything, the mom guilt was worse. My children are all grown, ultra-successful, and highly competent members of society, raising beautiful families of their own. Even when I reflect back on my parenting and things I could have done differently, I can take comfort in the fact that, in spite of my mistakes, my kids turned out pretty well.

My mama, however, is gone forever. There's no validation or feedback, no way of telling whether I did the right thing or even a good job. I drive myself crazy thinking of what more I could have done. The answer, of course, is nothing. I just wish that were more comforting.

It's going to take a lot of healing to let go of the guilt, and I know that healing is going to take time. At the end of her life, my mother was so much more than my mother. She was my baby, as helpless and vulnerable as an infant. Everything that happened to her fell on me, and whether or not that was completely fair is beside the point.

When another human being depends on you on such a deep level, you can't help but form a special bond. Babies, of course, grow up, and it's most every parents' prayer to see their child mature independently in their own right. But taking care of an elderly parent is like watching them age in reverse. The person you knew who was once so competent and strong—the one who scared away childhood monsters, the one you knew you could depend on no matter what— deteriorates into childlike helplessness. The fierceness I felt standing up for and defending my small children is the same fierceness I felt taking care of my mother in her old age. Her body betrayed her, and so did her mind. I was the only constant she had left.

I can't imagine a mother's pain when it comes to losing a young child. That's something I thank God I've never experienced, and by no means am I trying to compare losing Mama to what those mothers go through. Each pain, each situation, is different, and losing Mama *felt* different than any loss I'd ever felt before. She was completely reliant on me, which always makes me wonder if I made the right decisions and did the best for her.

Losing a parent comes with its own flavor of grief. But losing a parent who's helpless, completely vulnerable, and dependent on your every action and decision? That's something I was totally unprepared for. I'd always known my mother as my mama, but in my wildest dreams, I never could have predicted growing so close to her when she became my baby.

13

Saying Goodbye

We don't often think about rituals in modern society. The word "ritual" itself seems kind of old-fashioned, like a pagan religion or something out of a movie.

But just because the word sounds old doesn't mean we don't have rituals in our everyday lives. When we go to baby showers or a birthday party, we're taking part in a ritual, helping someone in our community transition from one stage of life to the next, be that motherhood or even retirement. Rituals give us built-in time and space to both celebrate and reflect on the past, present, and future. They're not sacred because they necessarily have anything to do with any divine guidance. They're sacred because we use them to help us make sense of change.

That's why we see similar sorts of rituals all around the world. Nearly every culture has a traditional marriage celebration or some way to celebrate the birth of a new child.

We also all seem to have some sort of ritual for death, some might even say the ultimate transition. Whether it's a funeral, a celebration of life, or an unwinding ceremony, there's not just expectations about how someone dies a "good death," we also put great amounts of effort into honoring that person after their soul has left their body. Nearly every culture, from Irish wakes to Hindu funeral pyres, has some sort of tradition when it comes to taking care of the dead. And if the dead aren't cared for properly, there are serious cultural consequences.

This brings up some important questions. If the person is dead, why make a big fuss over them? Why go to all that effort to give them a proper sendoff if you don't even believe they're in their body anymore?

If there's one thing Mama's funeral taught me, it's that death rituals aren't just for the one who's died. They're also for family and friends, for a greater community to make sense of loss. Here you are, living your life, and suddenly, someone who's always been there isn't there anymore. Of course, you know on the surface level that they've passed, but what does that *mean* in the greater scheme of things? To lose a neighbor? A father? A grandmother? A teacher or a congregation member? That person didn't just take up space. They were *a part of your life*. And now that they're gone, you're going to have to address that empty space.

Like I mentioned, grief and mourning doesn't look the same for everyone, and that's OK. Some people deal with those empty spaces faster and more smoothly than others. That's OK too. The point of a mourning ritual such as a funeral is that it gives you a period of time to start untangling all the complicated emotions. Without these rituals, people literally just "disappear"—*poof*, into thin air. That's not just disorienting, that's terrifying. If we don't take the time to honor and remember our dead, we, too, might just disappear someday. We spend our whole lives searching for meaning, building careers, families, and endeavors that leave the world different than the way we found it. Deep down, the real fear isn't that we're going to die. It's that the life we lived didn't matter.

Funerals aren't just some old-fashioned religious idea. They're essential rituals that help us make sense of what it means to be human—to be born, live, and then die. My mama and her family were always big fans of funerals, and though I didn't share their love of visitations and touching the corpses, I learned from a young age just how important it was to honor those who have passed.

And I wanted to honor my mama. If anyone deserved a full sendoff with all the bells and whistles, it was her. She'd spent so much of her life caring for others and helping everyone she knew. In life, she didn't care if people made a big fuss about her, but she *deserved* a big fuss. I wanted her to have that, especially as we celebrated her amazing life.

In typical Marsha fashion, I'd been planning my mama's funeral for years. This wasn't to be morbid or anything. I'm just a planner, and when someone gets that old and starts going downhill from dementia, you know what's going to happen. You'll have to make plans eventually. So why not get the details squared away earlier rather than later? I had twenty-six people in my immediate family, and then we'd have to plan for my brother's family, Mama's sisters, and everyone else back up in North Carolina. Travel plans were going to be hard enough as it was. There was no hurt in getting my ducks in a row.

My brother knows I've always been the planner of the family. I'd been collecting documents and pictures for years, including letters from Mama's friends and former Sunday school students. I had beautiful ribbons made to attach to flowers and plants, each one decorated with a loving message from a family member, and even commissioned a special pillow embroidered with her favorite Bible verses for her to rest her head. I picked out her outfit, her jewelry . . . everything I could.

Thank God I did that work beforehand. I wanted Mama's celebration to be so special because she was so special—the most special person I knew on Earth. I wanted her funeral to be the best celebration ever.

However, if there's one thing this whole experience taught me, it's that you can make all the plans you want, but God's the one in control. For a second, I thought about calling this book *Well, That's What I Get for Planning*. In Proverbs 16:9, it talks about man planning his ways even though the Lord directs his steps. I could have planned Mama's funeral five, ten years beforehand. It wouldn't have made a difference.

In my mind, I'd planned one of the good, old-fashioned funerals I'd grown up with. But this was the time of COVID, and funerals weren't looking anything like the ones I remembered. Florida was limiting crowds to fifty people, even outdoors, and we were lucky to have even that. In other geographical areas, things were even more restrictive. I've heard stories from people who didn't even get to have funerals for their loved ones.

Mama wanted to be buried beside Daddy in North Carolina, so we immediately started making plans to transport her body up north. Eddie wanted to have a visitation, but I didn't want to do that. He also wanted to have an open casket so our older, more traditional family members could see and touch her body. He was shocked when I pulled out all the materials I'd already prepared for the event. He had no idea I'd been planning for so long. I needed him to take charge of things in North Carolina, and he did. I am so grateful for that. Believe me when I say it's hard for me to let go of control, but Mama was already gone. Things had never been in my control to begin with.

At this point, everything kind of melts together in a blur of grief and exhaustion. You would think after all the stress of losing Mama, I would have just collapsed and slept for three weeks—especially considering that I also had COVID.

But no. Just like my mama, I kept pushing. There were still decisions and arrangements to be made. At one point, I came down with a horrible skin rash. Whether that was from stress, exhaustion, or maybe even a combination of everything, the doctor couldn't tell. *Getting in to see the doctor* ended up being way more stressful than the rash itself. I was having trouble breathing, and I was battling acid reflux, which I'd never had before in my life.

The long and short of it was that I was an absolute mess. It felt like everything was a mess. The end of Mama's suffering should have been a relief, but I just felt lost. Lost and tired. Tired and lonely. Lonely and guilty.

You can do an open casket only about two weeks after death, so we had to hurry to get everything together. I ended up being the one to deal with the funeral homes, scheduling the shipments and making sure the materials made their way up north. Then there was the body itself, transporting her from Florida all the way back to North Carolina, and after the shipments came the payments. I hired three separate pastors to speak at her service, then stayed up all night texting them stories, anecdotes, and details about Mama's life from me and my children. Then there were the obituaries, the clothes, and many details . . . time ticked away, and by the time I got my second negative COVID test, I was utterly depleted.

I didn't want to go back to North Carolina for reasons of my own. Family, as much as you love them, is complicated. And if there was one thing I didn't have at that time, it was extra strength and energy. Mama knew the situation, and we'd talked about it before she died. She never judged me or reprimanded me for it. She only ever listened with quiet kindness.

Then there was the issue of the virus. Strangely enough, my husband never tested positive, but Mama's caretaker Regina's husband was horribly sick in the hospital and nearly died. My brother and I were constantly texting back and forth about tests results. I was afraid to stay in a hotel, afraid to travel—afraid and exasperated by just about everything.

I was also worried about what other people would say about me if I didn't go to Mama's funeral. But that was just the thing. It wasn't about how I felt or what I needed. It was about what people would think about *me* if I wasn't there. Would they judge me? Would they even want me to come, knowing I had just recovered from COVID? At the time, it was too much to process.

I decided on May 16 that Gregg and I wouldn't be attending. After all the trauma of the last few weeks, the chaos of where to stay and how to work out the logistics . . . I just didn't have the energy. I also wasn't about to go up there and reopen old wounds.

There are consequences to not getting back up to North Carolina. Nobody knows that more than me. Whether my decision was right or wrong really doesn't matter. It was what it was. You could argue it was the safer, more respectful thing to do considering the times. You could also argue that it was cowardly and selfish. Two sides of the same coin.

But right or wrong, there are consequences for every decision we make. I didn't get the finality of seeing Mama's coffin put in the ground. I didn't cry with her sisters or sing hymns with the congregation that gathered. After so much time planning the ritual of my mother's funeral, I spent the whole day worrying from afar that everything would go right.

204 • GRIEF AND GRIT(S)

Mama was buried on May 20 at Westview Cemetery in Kinston beside Daddy. My journal entries from that day were painful. *We're in a COVID pandemic,* I wrote. *None of my family is going. So, so sad. I envisioned the biggest, grandest celebration of mom and had planned it for years. My heart aches that none of us are there.*

That day, it poured rain. There ended up being about fifty or sixty people, mostly my brother's friends or family members who'd heard by word of mouth. I'd made two separate videos for the event, one to be played during the service and another to play in the background during the visitation, and I recruited one of my cousins to read my remarks for me. The whole thing ended up being four pages about how kind, loving, and giving she was (most of the stories I included are already in this book), but it was the opening that really captured my feelings:

> *To my beautiful mama, from her baby,*
>
> *Everyone who knew Mama understands what a truly great person and faithful Christian she was. I would like to elaborate on what an amazing mother we were blessed to have. Of course, I have always known this about her, yet it was only after I began to take care of Mom that I started to look back at the details of the gentle, loving ways she mothered Eddie and me. Mom, please accept these words from my heart to yours as our forever bond . . .*

Even from a distance, I couldn't stop crying.

I was there in spirit and on FaceTime throughout the entire event (Lord only knows how we would have survived the pandemic without that technology). I still can't tell if that was a good idea or a bad one. While it was nice to attend in some small way, it was hard to be so far and, once again, so helpless.

My mother was always very particular about her hair. She used to cut her hair in our kitchen on top of working her full-time job. When my brother zoomed in his phone camera on the casket, I almost had a conniption. Her hair looked *horrible*. It was such a small thing, but it made me so angry. In life, she'd taken great pains to make sure her hair looked nice. She'd done mission work in the Philippines, and I'd wanted to play a video of Filipino children singing one of her favorite songs, but that didn't make it in either. Then her name was misspelled in the obituary . . .

Like I said, these seem like such small things looking back. But in the moment, the emotions were way too raw, like salt in an open wound. When you're tired and exasperated, the little things seem that much worse.

To me, it was all the stress of a wedding, a huge, elaborate party you host, but don't enjoy. I started thinking that it might be better to do something for my own immediate family, a smaller, more intimate memorial where we could say and do whatever we wanted in Mama's memory. So, once again, I put back on my planning hat to make it happen.

Part of it was trudging through grief. Part of it was relief at *finally* having something within my control. And

part of it was staying busy, cooking, preparing, and deco-
rating for visiting family. When you feel lost like that, it's
nice to have something you can micromanage—something
that feels familiar straight down the generational line.

It ended up being a good thing we didn't go to North
Carolina. The day after Mama was buried, my daughter
Lauren came again with her whole family. Schools were still
virtual, and she didn't want to stay in the heat of Atlanta.
We set up the kids' computers around the house and dove
right into a storm of cooking and grandparently entertainment. I shoved whatever grief I was wrestling straight back
down. Life moves on with or without you. It's the story of
my life—the story of my mother's life.

I love my children and my grandchildren. It was wonderful to have them with us, especially during such a lonely
and frightening time. COVID changed life in big ways, but
also in so many small ones. Meal trains, for instance. It's
standard protocol for our friends and family to put together
a meal train for a grieving household so they don't have
to cook. But there were no visitors, no casseroles. Nobody
could even hug me.

It wasn't like we had nothing to eat. What was missing
was the emotion, the ritual of it all. Little things like that
remind you that your community is still behind you, that
people you love are thinking of you and will be there to
support you. I don't think anyone could have ever imagined
how isolating and empty *not* having that community support would be. All over the world, people were dying of the

virus. And that very same virus was keeping them from the comfort and support their communities normally provide.

Funerals aren't just important because they honor the dead. They summon the strength of a community, friends and families alike.

Thankfully, my children were all able to come to the Florida memorial I held in Mama's honor. It was comforting to be able to plan and decorate the way I wanted, to give the event the attention to detail I thought Mama deserved. I printed out some of her signature quotes ("Pretty is as pretty does" and "Lord willing and the creek don't rise," just to name a few) to frame as well as pictures of her I hadn't sent to the North Carolina funeral. I even ordered shirts for the whole family with her picture on them, head tilted back, drinking her favorite Pepsi-Cola. I laid out her jewelry and her Bibles for her grandkids to choose from, and we commemorated all four generations with special portraits.

There was food and cake and all sorts of pink decorations—a real "fuss," just like I'd wanted. But even all the celebration didn't ease the loneliness like I'd hoped. I'd spent days on days, hour after hour painstakingly putting together a video about Mama's life. I don't know what I was expecting or what sort of catharsis I'd hoped to feel by showing it. My kids couldn't sit down and watch it all. Their kids were up and about, fidgeting, playing, fighting, crying, wrestling, and darting in and out of the room. It was completely unrealistic to expect everyone to sit through that, but it still unnerved me. Just this once, I wanted things to go right. I wanted *my* plan to work out.

But the funny thing was, Mama was there teaching me, even in those moments of quiet frustration and grief. She loved those kids. She wouldn't have been anything but graceful with them, even if they were being squirrely throughout her own video. She would have wanted them running around and playing, making a ruckus and having fun. That's just the kind of woman she was. Even in the midst of the pain and the grief, that thought hit me hard. As desperately as I tried, I couldn't do anything perfectly. And that was the way it was supposed to be. She was gently calling for me to let go, even in those moments of unspeakable loneliness.

That evening, we planted a palm tree on the beach in Mama's memory. Each grandchild took turns watering it, and we posted wooden angels around the trunk. Then we all headed down to the beach to release glowing lanterns. I'd written a prayer for the occasion, but I was too emotional to read it. Thankfully, my son took over for me.

> *Thank you, God, for this beautiful day that we could all be together as a family to celebrate the matriarch of our family. As a family, we loved, adored, and admired Mom, GrandMama, and Great Nine with all our hearts. She was such an example, Lord. She taught us about your love, your forgiveness, your grace and mercy, about family, marriage, and about salvation.*

As sad as we all are, we know that she is with you and sitting at your right hand, safe and secure in your arms. We thank you that she is no longer suffering, no longer scared and confused, and no longer lonely. We rejoice knowing that she is singing all the songs she loves with you and her old friends. We know we will be singing, too, one day with her! She is happy to finally see Dad, her mama, and her dad who she cried out for all the time.

We miss her so much and often question why, Lord, but we have peace knowing that you had a plan for her, and everything is in your time. Thank you, God, for giving her to us for ninety-one years and for all the memories we hold dear in our hearts that will never ever leave us. Thanks for holding my baby. Amen.

There was no rain that day, but as soon as my son uttered the final word, the strangest thing happened. A rainbow appeared on the horizon. I'd never seen anything like it in my life, and I doubt I'll see anything like it again. The photographer was able to snap a photo at just the right moment, and that picture will live forever in my heart. Every time I think about it, my eyes brim with tears. Nothing had gone the way I planned, but that sky was better than anything I could have ever imagined.

Let go, the rainbow seemed to say. Let go of the guilt. Let go of the expectations. Let go of control. Let go of the gut-wrenching grief that was eating me from the inside out.

Just let go.

As much as I wanted Mama's funeral and memorial to honor her, they both ended up just the way her life did—a selfless blessing to others.

The letters started pouring in after that, dozens upon dozens of them from people my mother had touched. They spoke of her kindness and her giving heart, the way she gave so selflessly to others and was always there when someone needed her. In the end, it wasn't any ceremony or party that honored my mother. It was the inflow of love for her, the gratitude of the people she served that graced her memory. I could throw galas and build a seven-foot-high statue in her honor, but nothing compares to the respect and adoration from the people she touched.

Even as I write this book, I know it won't serve to do her memory justice. It's only love—pure, Christlike love that drives us to put others before ourselves, take time out of our busy days to help someone in need, and put aside our own wants and desires for the sake of simple joys—that truly reflects the amazing life of Adaline Gray.

However, this doesn't mean I'm anywhere close to done making my fuss. As I write this book, my husband and I are in the process of donating a playground in her honor up on Black Mountain, North Carolina, at Cragmont Freewill Baptist Church Camp. The park will be called Adaline's Adventure Area, and I can only pray it brings as much laughter and light throughout the generations as my mother did all throughout her life. After all, she wouldn't have wanted any grand gala or fancy statue. If I know anything about my mama, I know she would have wanted a beautiful slice of nature where others could enjoy themselves, a welcoming place where children could have fun, and families could let go, if only for a little bit.

Maybe one day, I'll be sitting in the shade of that park, staring up through the golden sunlight, and I'll learn to let go too—if only for a little bit. I could never have imagined that saying goodbye to Mama would be just as hard as watching her leave us. Part of my heart still aches, grieving that her funeral and memorial weren't everything I'd planned, but that's also learning to let go of the part of me that feels guilty about everything else. There's a reason cultures all over the world have had mourning rituals since the beginning of time. Funerals give us an open invitation to explore these feelings, to process through the complexity and the loneliness. No amount of fuss, no matter how grand or opulent, can spare you from that.

The pandemic tipped our world upside-down, and I don't think we fully understand the ripple of impact it's made throughout this generation. There are many who weren't given the chance to mourn their loved ones—and many who didn't have the chance to have a funeral at all. This isn't just a matter of pomp and circumstance. Properly mourning and burying departed loved ones brings us together as families and unites us to our communities. It's not just about honoring the dead; it's about everyone coming together to remind you that you're not alone.

It's important to hold space for memories and for feelings no matter how good, bad, or painful they may be. We need rituals in our lives because transitions are an inescapable part of being human, and death is a part of that experience.

We need to make space for it. We need to make sense of it. We need to stand beside each other, even in the darkness of loss—because gosh darnit, that's what "grits and collards" folks like Mama always do.

Afterword

Nothing could have prepared us for COVID. Sure, we feel empathy for tragedy and mourn the aftermath of a natural disaster. But none of us have ever seen anything quite like the pandemic, something so far-reaching and impactful that it kept entire populations quarantined for months—in some places, over a year. It changed the way we think about public health, our communities . . . even ourselves.

Nothing prepares you for taking care of your elderly parents either. There's no manual or guidebook about how your relationship changes and the grueling decisions that lie ahead. No one comes around to tell you that your parent, maybe someone who's taken care of you your whole life, will decline slowly until they're as needy and helpless as a baby. And no one warns you that this kind of bond will be like nothing you've ever known.

Of course, everyone's experience is different. None of us will play the exact same role in caring for the elderly in our community or even our own family. But even if we don't have firsthand experience with these issues, it doesn't make them any less personal. Time ticks away just the same for all of us. Whether we want to think about it or not, we're all aging by the second. Eventually, every one of us is going to die.

My experience with Mama makes me want to be an advocate for old people, someone who goes in and helps give a voice to the voiceless. But the moment I get riled up about it, I deflate again. The issue is far more complicated than any amount of righteous anger. When it comes to advocacy for the elderly, how do you factor in familial wishes and responsibilities? Debilitating diseases such as dementia and Alzheimer's? A global pandemic that disproportionately affects the elderly?

I mentioned in the beginning of the book that I don't have answers to these hard questions, and that's OK. Just because we don't have a magical solution doesn't mean we shouldn't open up the conversation. Looking back at Mama's life, the beginning and middle as well as the bitter end, is a look at how we treat human beings in our society. As a culture, we're age-averse; we have an entire multibillion-dollar industry devoted to staying youthful. No one wants to talk about the consequences of growing old in our modern world, but growing old is exactly what we're doing every second of every day.

I cringe when I think about the way my mother was so easily cast off at the end of her life. It makes me wonder what's in store for me and my husband as we begin to decline. Of course, we're blessed with means, wonderful children, and access to a lot of options others aren't. But through my family, my mama also had all these things, and her death was still a nightmare. It didn't matter how much money you had, how famous you were, or which side of the tracks you came from. Somehow, some way, COVID decimated our lives.

It's easy to focus on those last few months, to let the grief and the sadness eclipse all the joy and inspiration Mama brought to others throughout her life. In 2022, on the anniversary of her death, I woke up with horrible nightmares. All the running around, pleading with doctors, realizing she was so horribly sick, begging for someone to help her . . .

Even now, some nights I wake up sobbing. Other nights I don't sleep at all.

Those memories still haunt me, and there's physical trauma in those memories. I was so stressed after Mama died that I developed an ulcer. I can't help but think that if COVID hadn't happened, she would still be alive. Maybe she would have lived to ninety-five, ninety-seven . . . with the right medicine and care, maybe even over one hundred. The number doesn't matter as much as the dream that she would still be with me, my precious baby, and with the rest of her grandchildren and great-grandchildren who loved her so much. I guess it all goes back to my desire for control, to be everything for everyone just like Mama.

It's hard to make sense of all these complex emotions, especially when they're swirling in my head like a hurricane. Grief, anger, nostalgia, helplessness . . . even the love I had for my baby was strong, so pure, it's difficult to put into words. But that's when I have to pause and go back to the beginning, to return to the pictures, the journals, and all the stories of my mother and her childhood. Mama wasn't just a number. She wasn't just another elderly COVID victim. She was a real woman with real stories, a woman who gave everything she had to other people, for better or for worse. She was a beautiful soul and not a number. When people ask me how old she was when she died, the answer of ninety-one isn't usually followed with condolences or even sympathy. More often than not, the response is a half-hearted *oh*, as if reaching a certain age makes up for all the pain.

Far too often, I find myself lost in all the negative emotions. When I stop to think about what I've learned from this experience, the first word that comes to mind is mistrust, mostly toward our medical system and those who claim to do good. Of course, there were heroes and villains. And of course, even those labels are far too simple to slap on someone as a judgment. But then I think about the medical workers in Mama's story, the ones who'd taken an oath, and the red-hot bitterness rises up again. What do you do when you have nowhere to turn? When your doctor won't care for you, when hospice won't admit you? What do you do when the people who are supposed to be there aren't anymore? My mama showed up for everyone in their time of need. It breaks my heart to think of all the people who let us down.

But it isn't fair to focus on those people either. There were plenty of heroes in this story, from Regina, who stayed by Mama's side until the very end, to Javier, the nurse who almost lost his job because he wouldn't quit on us. Then there was Brittany who didn't bat an eyelash about leaving her children and coming to help. Without her, things would have been so much worse. It's so easy to get lost in the betrayal and forget that so many amazing heroes were holding us up through everything.

But what about the thousands in this country who don't have family to support them? A community to stand behind them or a good doctor to be their advocate? COVID isn't just a learning lesson. It's a challenge to take a good, hard look at the way we treat our elderly population. As a society, we need to define our responsibility to them, not only for the present, but for the sake of our own futures. Our population is aging faster than we can keep up. How are we going to handle that? How do *we* want to be handled when we get there? If seniors are so easily cast off and triaged during a national emergency, is it any wonder we're so terrified of getting old?

In the book of Matthew, Jesus tells his followers to be as wise as snakes and innocent as doves. That paradox has always baffled me. Here we are being told to be shrewd and calculating, but also gentle and guileless. How can you be both at once? All my life, I watched people take advantage of my mother, a mother I longed for but also struggled to live up to. She would go to help someone at the drop of a hat. I never heard her say, "I'm sorry, I can't," or "This is a bad time." It drove my daddy nuts. I felt like, because of everyone else, I never truly had my mom present for me when I was a child.

So I became a planner, meticulous and calculating, supervising every little thing down to the last detail. While raising five kids, it might have been the only thing that kept me sane. But it also fed into this crushing sense of guilt, guilt that I could never be as saintly as Mama and that no matter how hard I tried, my plans would always fall through.

Is it better to be the serpent or the dove? Trusting or gullible? Selfless or safe? Mama was the most Christlike woman I knew. Part of it was her inborn nature; part of it was her faith. But that was the irony of it. To be more like Jesus means following in his footsteps, even if that means taking up a cross and martyring yourself. Would you live your life selflessly knowing that no one would be with you in your time of need? Could Mama have ever imagined that when she called to me when she was helpless, beckoning me from behind her screen door, I wouldn't go in to see her?

I still remember the look on her face when I told her I couldn't go in. She didn't cry. She didn't scream or beg for help. At that point, she probably didn't understand what was going on or why I had to keep my distance, but she nodded her head as much as she could. Her face was sad, but her eyes were quiet. *OK*, she seemed to say, and I have to imagine what Jesus's face would have looked like, alone up there on the cross. But I'm not like my mama. I certainly can't accept everything, least of all a lonely death, as a part of God's will.

It kills me that I didn't go into that room to see her after we'd both received our positive tests. The guilt of it still poisons me from the inside out, and it makes me wonder if I can truly blame anyone for failing me when I feel like I failed Mama. Do we get to hold onto anger while giving others grace? Here I am, angry at these doctors, when I was too scared to go in and see her. Am I actually angry at them? Or am I still unable to forgive myself for the way things went?

There are no easy answers to those questions either. All we can do is keep working through them day by day. I know I'm not alone in losing an elderly parent, and I know I'm not the only one struggling with these feelings. I also know very personally what happened in health care facilities throughout the pandemic, and I know that we still have a long way to go in healing our collective trauma.

That's why it's so important to share these stories, to talk about what happened and wade through the aftermath, no matter how ugly and grief-stricken it may be. We're living in the wake of tremendous loss, a generation that experienced death, isolation, and desperation on a massive scale. My mother's story may be one of a million, but it's also important. We have to keep these records, to truly step back to figure out what happened and how we can do better.

My mama was always my teacher. Whether it was teaching me to bake, wash feet, recite Bible stories in Sunday school, or be patient with my children as we drove back and forth from Florida, she was passing on lessons in not only what she said, but also in the way she lived. As she aged back into childhood and went from my mother to my baby, she never stopped teaching me. And even now that she's gone, the lessons just keep going.

The anger and bitterness I have toward those who failed me reflect my own guilt over failing her. My attempts to plan and stay in control come from a place of deep, dark fear. My disappointment toward others has shown me so much about my own expectations, and my grief is a testament to just how fiercely I loved her. Even through all of this, I know she's patient with me, smiling down from heaven on the good days and the bad. She loved everyone, sinners and saints alike, for exactly who they were, wherever they happened to be. And I know she's still up there loving me for exactly who I am, no matter how far I have to go or how much I have left to learn.

As I wind up this last chapter, I realize that my mama's life is a beautiful, never-ending lesson. Lanie Adaline Gray, from mother to baby and beyond, has been my greatest teacher. She's taught me about seasons, about what it means to truly be present in every stage in life, and how your love for someone can change over time. She taught me about roles, responsibilities, and obligations—courage, compassion, and what it truly means to be a family. Between selflessness and selfishness, self-care and self-sacrifice, there's so much to be learned. And it's not about being right or wrong, good or bad. It's simply about *loving* and *living*, about doing the best you have right where you're at with everything you have.

Ultimately, my mother has (and still is) teaching me that two things can be true at once. I can commemorate, honor, and love Adaline as a light and a joy. I can treasure my memories around her and smile every time I think about her drinking a Pepsi-Cola or driving with two feet. Whenever I see a rainbow, I know it's her. I make her biscuits and heart-shaped cakes. I have carried on the tradition of having a Happy Birthday, Jesus cake at Christmastime. Each of these is seemingly small, but very powerful and significant in helping us keep her memory alive.

I can also feel anger and indignance over what happened to her. I can mourn the end of her life just as I can mourn my own shattered plans. You have to feel the brokenness in order to put yourself back together again. To grieve someone is a reminder of just how much they meant to you.

Mama lives on in my heart in so many ways, and as long as she keeps teaching, I'll never stop learning. The *couldas, shouldas, wouldas* still lurk in the past, but so do all the bright, wonderful memories, the joys that keep me present and give me incredible hope for the future.

On Mother's Day, May 14, 2023, we dedicated Adaline's Adventure Area at Cragmont in Black Mountain, North Carolina. In many ways, it was the funeral we didn't get to have, with family and friends attending from near and far. People spoke about the influence Mama had on their lives, we released butterflies, drank sweet tea, and ate Southern food, all while the children played on the playground. It was a joyous remembrance.

My mother, my baby, is still with me as all she is and all she ever was. That's a love that nothing—not even death—could ever take away. So, Mama, I will see you in heaven some day—Lord willing and the creek don't rise.

Acknowledgments

This book wouldn't be possible without so much love from so many.

God—For his presence, love, and comfort during the difficult process of reliving Mama's life and death.

Grandaddy Gray—Who taught me the importance of journaling and gave me a love for the written word.

Daddy—For showing me strength, courage, and gentleness all at the same time.

Big Gregg—Who has listened to "I could write a book" a million times and being there for me with love and support when I finally did. Thanks for being my biggest cheerleader.

Hannah—Thank you for helping me honor my mother in such a beautiful way.

Camille—Thank you for championing my book.

Sofia—For the little shove that got the ball rolling.

Eddie—For having a good memory and taking me back to some great times.

Kay and Alice—For taking phone calls day or night with lots of questions.

My Children—For lovingly believing I could pull this off, then being surprised when I finally did.

My Grandchildren—For always putting a smile on Great Nine's face.

Stephanie—For being there for me every step of the way.

Dr. Chen—For giving me continuous energy and herbs.